Time Out
for tots, teens
and everyone in between

How to get your children
to do as they're told

GW00644786

Time Out
for tots, teens
and everyone in between

How to get your children
to do as they're told

RANDOM HOUSE
NEW ZEALAND

Diane Levy

National Library of New Zealand Cataloguing-in-Publication Data
Levy, Diane.
Time out for tots, teens and everyone in between / Diane Levy.
Includes index.
ISBN 978-1-86941-945-5
1. Discipline of children. 2. Child rearing. 3. Parenting.
I. Title.
649.64—dc 22

A RANDOM HOUSE BOOK
published by
Random House New Zealand
18 Poland Road, Glenfield, Auckland, New Zealand
www.randomhouse.co.nz

First published 2007

Text design: Anna Seabrook
Cover design: Katy Yiakmis
Printed in New Zealand by Geon Group

To all my family, friends, colleagues and clients
who tolerate my absence in their lives
while I write and whom I trust
to welcome me back again

CONTENTS

INTRODUCTION:
WHY WRITE A BOOK
ABOUT TIME OUT?

And so I ask myself the question, 'Diane, why are you writing another book? What do you think that you have to offer? What can you possibly say that hasn't already been said by you or by your colleagues — people of goodwill and knowledge whose only desire is to help parents in their quest to parent pleasantly and more effectively?'

PARENTING IS STILL A STRUGGLE FOR MANY OF US

I have decided to write another book because parents are still struggling with getting their toddlers to carry out simple instructions like:

- *'Hold still while I dress you.'*
- *'Come to Mummy so I can put on your jacket.'*
- *'Leave the cat alone!'*

Parents of school-age children are still struggling with:

- *'Stop tormenting your brother.'*
- *'Hurry up! We are going to be late for school.'*
- *'Do you have to argue about everything?'*

Parents of teens are still struggling with:

- *'I've asked you ten times to give me a hand with the dishes and you still haven't shown up.'*
- *'Why is the whole family sitting in the car waiting for you?'*
- *'I tell you where I am going and when I plan to be back. Why can't you do the same for me?'*

While these behaviours are annoying and make family life rather difficult, when I sit and talk with parents for a while, there is one factor — over and above the actual behaviour — that is the most upsetting for parents.

WHAT UPSETS PARENTS THE MOST?

What upsets parents the most is when they find themselves no longer enjoying their children's company.

When children are difficult to manage, when they are rude and disrespectful, when they cannot tolerate the least frustration without a loud and unpleasant meltdown, it is jolly hard to keep liking them. I am not saying for a single moment that we stop loving them, but liking them is another matter. I think that we owe it to our children to raise them as pleasant, productive individuals whose company we — and everyone else who comes into contact with them — can enjoy.

WHY TIME OUT?

I am still counselling parents one-on-one in private practice who have read my books, been to my seminars and seen my TV series, *Demons to Darlings*. They like what I have to say, they find me credible and yet, when they try to put into practice the information and ideas that they have gleaned, it isn't working. Often they say, 'We've tried Time Out. It isn't working' or 'We have tried Time Out but he is getting too heavy to drag there' or 'We used Time Out when he was little but now he is too old'.

When I work with parents individually, we almost always wind up using an age-appropriate Effective Time Out that leads to a positive change in their child's behaviour.

WHAT DO YOU MEAN
BY EFFECTIVE TIME OUT?

When I talk about Time Out, I do *not* mean hauling off your child to the coal cellar with the spiders. I do not mean sitting them on the naughty chair. I don't mean sending them to their room for hours of isolation, and I don't mean timing isolation in some relationship with their ages.

So what do you mean, Diane? I think of Time Out as a way of showing our children that — for reasonable requests and reasonable expectations of appropriate behaviour — we mean what we say. Time Out is a way of showing our children that, once we have made a request, nothing much in the way of goods or services from us is going to happen until that is done.

Furthermore, there are certain behaviours that we have already made clear we find unacceptable. When these behaviours occur, we can use Time Out as a means of showing our children not only that we disapprove of that behaviour, but that we have absolute faith that they can do the right thing and stop themselves from doing the wrong thing.

This book will show you how to use Time Out in a way that ensures that our child is not struggling with us. Instead, we will set up Time Out in such a way that our children struggle *only with themselves* until they can resolve the dilemma: 'I don't want to do that; I know I have to do that.' This is a life lesson that all of us need to deal with. One mark of a self-disciplined person is one who can make themselves do necessary tasks that they would rather not do.

Traditional	Effective
Punishes bad behaviour	Empowers the child to self-correct his behaviour
Is something a parent does **to** a child	Is something a parent does **for** the child
Often invites resentment	Leads to the child learning to tolerate the ordinary frustrations of life
Control of duration rests with the parent	Control of duration rests with the child
Can only be used if you are strong enough to get the child to the Time Out spot	Does not require a physical battle
Is only as good as the Time Out spot you have available	Can be used anywhere
Would rarely be an option for teens	Is the ideal way for managing teens
Requires huge parental effort	Requires relatively little effort

Instead of exhausted and angry parents battling with rebellious and angry children, we need to create an environment where our children only battle with their own unwillingness.

Furthermore, I want us to develop ways of leading our children on the path to self-discipline without having to resort to punishment.

WHAT'S WRONG WITH PUNISHMENT?

Punishment works really well for 'good' children. It doesn't work nearly as well for children who are inclined towards rebellion.

Think of it in adult terms. I imagine that you are a good, law-abiding citizen who has the odd traffic infringement. You carelessly run a red light. A few days later a traffic infringement notice arrives. You practise your Anglo-Saxon for a while, say a number of rather unkind things about the police force, the law, the government and the inanimate camera that snapped your folly. You try to think up an excellent reason why you alone should be exempt from the consequences of your action . . . and eventually you grudgingly write out a cheque and post it. Furthermore, without having actually met you, I am prepared to guarantee that you will stop at every red light for at least the next three months.

In other words, a person who is naturally inclined to do the right thing rather than the wrong thing responds well to a consequence or punishment when they stray from accepted behaviour. They learn from the negative aspects of the experience and opt for the pro-social choice.

On the other hand, if you have no respect for the law, if you never respond to traffic infringement notices, if you never pay a traffic fine or only pay one as an absolutely last resort to avoid jail, the idea of someone imposing a punishment or consequence on you tends to make you fight your responsibility rather than own it. You tend to behave as if it is unfair that anyone should dare to impose their will upon you and you are determined to fight them 'to the death' to get out of it.

If backed into a corner, you may well submit to a consequence or punishment, but you grump and growl about how unfair it is and you refuse to acknowledge to yourself that it is your fault. You learn very little from the experience other than the practice of holding a grudge and plotting revenge.

Punishing children works for the good ones

When we impose a punishment (or a consequence — which is just a punishment dressed up in politically correct clothing), it will work well for the relatively co-operative child. They understand that they have done wrong. They accept the consequences of their actions. They either don't like incurring their parents' wrath or they don't like what happened as a result — or both. They decide that they will not do that again. Punishment works for good children.

But what about our difficult-to-manage child? What about the child who doesn't seem to learn from our disapproval or anger? What about the child who doesn't seem to care that they are upsetting us? What about the child who appears indifferent to the removal of privileges or the child who apparently doesn't care about stars, stickers, pocket money or possessions?

When we use punishment on our angry, rebellious children we tend to invite further anger, further rebellion and lingering resentment. We get involved in a battle of wills where we are always having to think up better, bigger and brighter punishments (or consequences, if you are more comfortable with that term) and, instead of our child responding to our efforts, their resentment and anger keeps growing and they look for ways to punish us back.

When we find ourselves in this sort of vicious cycle, we wind up demeaning our child and demeaning ourselves.

WHY EFFECTIVE TIME OUT?

I firmly believe that Time Out — in the ways shown in this book —

is a powerful and useful strategy for all ages. I think it is a respectful and dignified way for parents to keep out of the traps of arguing, nagging, cajoling and bribing. When we use Effective Time Out, we don't have to get caught up in a cycle of explaining, reasoning, yelling and punishing.

When our children are willing to listen to our instructions and carry them out, they are more likely to respect us enough to turn to us when they are worried or upset. When they have respect for us, they are more likely to come to us for advice. Once we have relatively co-operative children, we can relax about their behaviour and really enjoy their company.

What is the most frequent way we, as parents, go wrong with traditional Time Out?

The biggest mistake we, as parents or educators, make is to use Time Out as a punishment. Often we find ourselves using the language of punishment:

- *'If you do that again, I'll give you a Time Out.'*
- *'If you don't do as I've asked, you'll have to have a Time Out.'*
- *'I've already warned you twice. You know you don't hit your brother. Time Out for you, young man.'*

If we use Time Out in this way, we are just as likely to incur the same sort of rebellion and resentment as with any other sort of punishment.

A more effective way of using Time Out

Instead, I would like us to use Effective Time Out as a way of teaching our children that they are capable of making better choices and wiser decisions. Let's use Time Out in such a way that our children can change their minds and choose a better way of behaviour, that they can choose the pro-social way rather than the anti-social way, and that they can retain their integrity and individuality while conforming to reasonable norms of behaviour.

Most importantly, I would like to see us, as parents, guiding our children to being well-rounded adults capable of saying 'No' to dangerous and distasteful situations and 'Yes' to all the wonderful opportunities life has to offer.

In this book, I would like to offer you a printed part of the journey that parents take in one-on-one counselling. Even though a book can never have the same interactional quality as face-to-face counselling, I welcome the chance to help you change your way of thinking about Time Out so that you can use it — and its opposite, Emotional Support — in such a way that you raise a pleasant child whose company you can enjoy.

Let's go!

Note: The English language seems to be missing a few expressions that I need it to have

A word for all ages

Since this book is designed for tots, teens and everyone in between, I am struggling for a single word that conveys the age range between newborn and independent young adulthood, i.e. around twenty.

Since this is a parenting book, I take it as read that the young people we are talking about are in our care and under our responsibility (whether the reader is a parent, a teacher, a caregiver or a family member other than a parent) and I think it is useful to think of them as our 'child' or our 'children'.

Hence, when you read the word 'child' or 'children', I mean it to imply whatever age child (newborn to twenty) you have in mind at that particular moment.

A word for all genders (children)

In the singular, the English language lacks pronouns that mean 'male and female' or 'male or female'. It is too cumbersome to spend an entire book writing 'he or she' or 'his or hers'.

Irrespective of what gender pronoun is written, I am referring to both boys and girls unless I specify a particularly girly or boyish trait.

Hence, when you read the words he, she, his or hers, I mean it to imply whichever gender child (newborn to twenty) you are thinking of at that particular moment.

Where I cannot express things fluently without resorting to a gender-specific pronoun, you can expect to find 'she' and 'hers' in all odd-numbered chapters and 'he' and 'his' in all even-numbered chapters.

A word for all genders (parents)

'Parent' is a great word that covers both mother and father. However, when I am illustrating how we might talk to young children, I often refer to the parent in the third person. How come?

When our babies are small they do not perceive themselves as separate from their mothers. As many parents, grandparents and caregivers will testify, most babies under eight months will 'go to anyone'. Often it feels like suddenly, around the nine-month mark, they understand precisely what it means when Mum hands them over; they really notice and many of them let us know in no uncertain terms. (The technical term is 'individuation'.)

Apparently, one of the things that we unconsciously do to verbally aid this individuation is speak to our young babies and children using the third person. Hence we automatically say phrases like, 'Come to Mummy. Come to Daddy.'

If I am using these phrases to illustrate a point, particularly if I am referring to 'our' children, I have real difficulty thinking about myself as 'Daddy'. So I apologise in advance to dads who are reading this and ask you to do the mental leap that 'Mummy', in this context, refers to parents of either gender.

Considering all the other things we have to worry about as we try to raise our children to become civilised, independent young adults, asking you to make these inferences will be the least of all our worries.

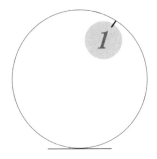

WHERE DOES
TIME OUT FIT
INTO PARENTING?

The question I am most frequently asked is, 'How do I get my children to do as they are told?' That question may come disguised as another question or statement:

- *'How can I get her to show more respect?'*
- *'She seems to have so much anger inside her.'*
- *'The least thing sets her off.'*
- *'There doesn't seem to be anything I can do to make her happy.'*
- *'Homework is a nightmare.'*

- *'I am worried about her self-esteem.'*
- *'They rang me up to say she has bitten another child at kindy and can I take her home.'*
- *'She never tells me where she is going.'*

However the question is presented, it almost always boils down to one issue. 'If only s/he would do as s/he is told, we wouldn't have a problem.'

So where does the issue of compliance to simple, ordinary parenting requests fit into the whole picture of raising our children?

THE FOUR STRANDS OF PARENTING

I find it easiest to think about parenting in terms of four developmental strands running from the time a baby is born till the age of about twenty. Not that our children have necessarily left home — for the last time, anyway — by the time they are twenty. But, by the time they are twenty and if they are still at home, I would expect us to be living with a relatively independent young person who has all the attributes necessary to live as an adult.

As parents we are responsible for making sure our children achieve or acquire:

1   emotional independence

2   self-discipline

3   skills

4   morality.

The path to emotional independence

When our babies are little, they have very little capacity to handle their feelings and tend to be overwhelmed by negative ones. So when they are distressed, our first inclination is to remove the cause of their distress. We change them, feed them, burp them, give them a change of scenery — in other words, we do our best to remove the cause of their distress.

Emotionally independent

Increasing ability
to tolerate
ordinary
frustrations

Emotionally dependent

If we cannot seem to find the cause and remove it, we do something else to help them deal with their feelings. We walk around with them, at a rhythmical pace, muttering our own version of (I seem to remember this as my walking mantra for our third child) 'There, there. Mummy loves you. Daddy loves you. Robbie loves you. Tanny loves you. Everybody loves a Deborah.' And we repeat this, while pacing, for as long as it takes to settle our baby.

What is going on here? The explanation that most resonates with me is that, at moments of distress, our babies are full of negative energy that needs to be discharged. By walking and patting and muttering, we somehow enable them to discharge their comparatively small amount of negative energy into our much larger body. We, being larger, can absorb that amount of energy without it destroying our equilibrium.

I like to think about it as the effect of adding a teaspoon of hot water to a large cup of cold water. The large cup of water would scarcely notice the difference. This model hold up nicely when we are dealing with the child whose distress goes on and on and on and we don't seem to be able to alleviate it. Several teaspoons of hot water do start to make a difference to the temperature of a cup of cold water. We are geared to find our babies' crying distressful and if we are unable to help, we eventually find ourselves very stressed.

Helping our children along the path

As our children mature emotionally, they become more and more capable of handling their feelings. It is amazing how often 'Mummy kiss it better' solves a whole lot of problems when you're a toddler.

As our children get older, they need to tell us about their upsets and often by our listening and empathising and offering a hug, the problem will be solved. As they move into their teen years, provided we can keep our listening skills up and our criticising turned down, we can still be one of the people our children turn to when they have a problem. However, it is natural for them to be turning to their peers for support as well.

It is the mark of an emotionally mature person not that they don't have their feelings, not that they suppress their feelings, but that they can experience their full range of feelings — happy, sad, delighted, outraged, furious, upset — in socially appropriate ways. Further, it is the mark of an emotionally mature person that, when they are overwhelmed by negative feelings, they will turn for help to other adults to listen to them, to support them and to assist their problem solving.

Tolerating ordinary frustrations

It is the mark of emotionally mature adults that they can tolerate the ordinary frustrations of life without avoidance or meltdown. When we use the term 'emotionally immature' about an adult, we usually mean that they behave in a childishly impulsive or volatile way. So what does 'emotionally immature' mean when we refer to a child? It means that they are handling their emotions in a way that we would expect of a much younger child.

When I speak with parents who are struggling with a child's behaviour but are having difficulty expressing just what is the problem, one leading question I often ask is, 'Does she have trouble handling the ordinary frustrations of life?' An answer like, 'She just seems to fly off the handle at the least little thing' means that we are dealing with a child who has less emotional maturity than we would expect at that age. Put another way, her capacity to tolerate the ordinary frustrations of that age is less than is appropriate.

Two-year-old 'wobblies' are to be expected in a two-year-old. They are a mark of emotional immaturity in a ten-year-old. A five-year-old may struggle when she cannot win a game. We expect our eight-year-olds to be getting to grips with the concept of being both a gracious winner and a gracious loser.

As our children learn to handle the ordinary age-appropriate frustrations of life, they progress up the path from emotionally dependent to emotionally independent. We don't want to be taking the frustration away, neither do we want the frustration to be unbearable for our children.

Our job as parents is to support them as they meet these ordinary frustrations so that they learn to handle them. It is also our job to guard them from the frustrations that are dangerous or unbearable.

STRAND TWO

The path to self-discipline

Richard Gordon, who wrote the *Doctor in the House* series, described a baby as 'a very short person with no discipline at either end'. It is our task, as parents, to take these very short, undisciplined people and help them grow up to be taller, self-disciplined young adults.

Notice that I say 'self-disciplined' rather than simply 'disciplined'. 'Discipline' is not sufficient to prepare them for the adult world. It simply does not serve our children well enough to learn to do as they are told, provided there is a responsible person who is watching. Eventually, we need them to become not just disciplined, but self-disciplined.

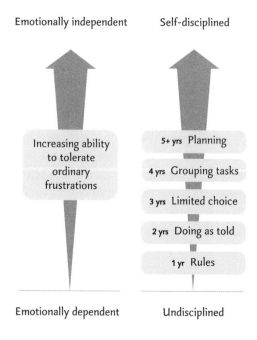

The pathway to becoming self-disciplined is a five-step process:

First year of life — just do it

1   One year old — household rules

2   Two years old — accepting imposed discipline
(doing as told)

Just do it

When our babies are little we have the power to do with them as we please. If the child is in one room and we wish them to be in another room, we just take them there. If it is the time of day when we think our baby needs a bath, we put the baby in the bath. If we wish our baby to wear a jacket, we put the baby in a jacket.

Just in case we are carried away with our incredible power, there are many things we cannot make our baby do. We cannot make a wide-awake baby sleep, we cannot make a non-hungry baby eat and we have very little control over when they wee or poo. (For the record, I do know the words 'urinate' and 'defecate'. They just feel too medical and not 'user-friendly' enough when we are talking about the body functions of a baby or small child.)

Step 1: Complying with household rules

By the time our children are one year old, they are capable of understanding that there are certain things they are not allowed to do. Picture the scene:

Our ten-month-old crawler heads for the curtains. At this age, that would be perfectly normal exploratory behaviour. A ten-month-old cannot tell what the curtain feels like, tastes like or smells like, without the actual experience of touching, mouthing and sniffing. Further, looking at the curtain from the front, our little crawler has no idea what it looks like from the other side.

We may or may not allow the exploratory behaviour, but sooner or later we say, 'Leave the curtains alone', lift up our crawler, take her a short distance away and give her something else to do.

One such experience will not be enough to teach our crawler to leave the curtains alone, so she will repeat the experience several times — and several times we will gently admonish our child and take her away to do something else.

The look

I am often asked, 'When is a child old enough for discipline?' That sounds like a pretty grim question to ask about a little one-year-old, so I prefer to rephrase it, 'When is a child old enough to understand that there are certain rules?' My answer is, 'When they are old enough to give you *the look*.'

This is the sort of look you may get from a one-year-old. She has repeatedly crawled to explore the curtains. You have repeatedly removed her and explained or growled that this is not on.

One day, she heads towards the curtains. As she is about to pull on the curtains, she pauses — possibly hand on curtain — and looks back with a grin. 'The look' says 'I know I am not supposed to do this, but I intend to anyway.' Depending on your style of child, 'the look' may also be saying, 'I am so cute and adorable that you will let me get away with this.'

Once your child is sophisticated enough to give you 'the look', you know that she fully understands the concept of rules. She understands that there are some things that she is not supposed to do.

Tolerating ordinary frustrations — again

As our children learn that there are some things they are simply not allowed to do, they learn to tolerate the frustrations of not being allowed to do them and to give up on the idea that they can.

Through the pathway to self-discipline they will come up against this 'I want to; I know that I shouldn't' again and again. Through meeting this and conforming to reasonable norms of behaviour, they learn to tolerate the ordinary frustrations of life — a skill that will stand them in good stead as they confront the difficulties that inevitably crop up on the path to becoming and being adults.

Am I crushing their spirit?

'Am I crushing their spirit?' is a question that I am asked again and again and again when it comes to matters of discipline. My reply is 'Absolutely not.' When we talk about the pathway to self-discipline — and particularly when we are talking about things like household rules and doing as told — we are talking about compliance to simple instructions like 'Hold still while I put on your nappy', 'Leave the cat alone', 'Please come and set the table', 'We need to be ready to leave the house in ten minutes'.

In no way am I suggesting that we quell their spirits. They need to be free to dance and sing and learn and play and work in their own way. We need to foster their independence and their self-esteem and their creativity and their individual personality.

This in no way contradicts the social need to be part of a family and part of a society and to conform to simple requests like 'Put your socks on', 'Draw on the paper', 'It's time to get your homework done', 'Getting home by 11pm would be reasonable tonight'.

Step 2: Doing as told

Somewhere between one and two years, our children start to challenge us when we ask them to do something or to stop doing something. For them, this is an important developmental step. It is also a step with inherent contradictions. On the one hand, it is important that our children become individuated. It is important that they continue the process of becoming individuals, separate from their parents and capable of having their own thoughts, opinions and independent actions. On the other hand, they need to become members of the society that they live in and conform to many of the norms that this society asks of them.

By doing what is expected of them, they learn to fit in — to accept imposed discipline.

Step 3: Limited choice

By the time our children are three, we need to be offering them limited choices. Begin with a choice of two things: 'Do you want Weetbix or cornflakes?', 'Are you going to wear your red sweatshirt or your green sweatshirt?'. When we offer choice, we are teaching our children commitment. We are also tugging on their ability to tolerate the frustration of leaving a choice behind.

When they commit to Weetbix, they are also committing to the frustration of leaving cornflakes behind — for that day, anyway. Committing to a choice is an important life skill.

By giving them lots of opportunity to have limited choice, by giving them the chance to commit to a choice and try it out and to evaluate whether it was a good idea or not, we are setting them up to learn to make wise choices and stick with them as they begin to encounter the dangerous choices of adolescence and adulthood, when they really count.

Step 4: Grouping tasks

By the time our child is four, they are capable of holding three or four 'compliances' in their head and tolerating the frustration of completing them. We can say to them, 'We are leaving the house soon. Brush your teeth. Brush your hair and put your lunch in your lunch box.'

At kindergarten, their teachers can say, 'Now everyone tidy up before mat-time', and our children can self-generate several tasks that they see need doing. They may put the blocks back on the shelf, then look around to see if any puzzles need putting away and then pick up any scrap paper that has been left lying around. (Of course, many of us parents may have to deal with the fact that they can do this willingly and without fuss at kindergarten while proving entirely incapable of managing much less than the equivalent at home.)

Step 5: Planning

Out of this ability to group three or more tasks together comes the increasing ability to plan and execute that plan. This requires our child to break down a larger task into smaller tasks, choose a suitable order to do them in and then have the self-discipline to carry them through.

When our children can do this easily and often, they are well along the pathway to becoming self-disciplined young adults.

The path to being skilled

With all due respect to our beautiful newborn babies, they do start off relatively unskilled. Over their first twenty years — and hopefully for the rest of their life — they need to be continuously learning new skills and increasing their established skills base. When we use the term 'skilled' in the context of child-rearing, we are talking about our children learning all the skills that they need to be an independent adult.

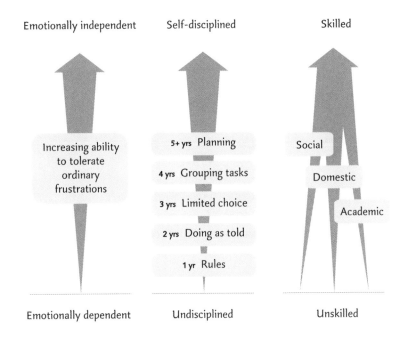

We can divide these skills into three categories:

1   Social skills

2   Domestic skills

3   Academic skills.

We are aiming to raise an independent young adult who has the foundation for all the social skills, domestic skills (a broad range covering self-care, running a household, managing transport, managing finances, finding and maintaining work, organising their time and resources) and academic skills (those learned at primary, secondary and tertiary institutions or through home schooling and self-directed learning).

The path from being amoral

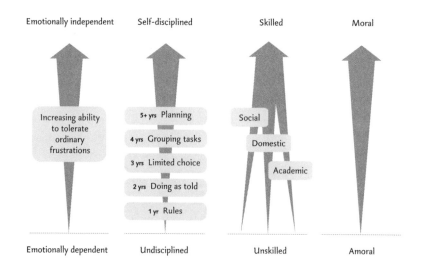

All our babies begin as amoral beings. By the time we get our children to twenty, we want them to have all the values, all the virtues and all the morals to make their way ethically in the adult world. We also need them to be developing and growing their spirituality — some belief that there is a greater force than themselves. This of course may only come after adolescence when they may well experience themselves as the force around which the world revolves.

So where do we start?

I believe that teaching and supporting our children to tolerate the ordinary frustrations of life and progress along the pathway to becoming emotionally independent leads to their developing self discipline.

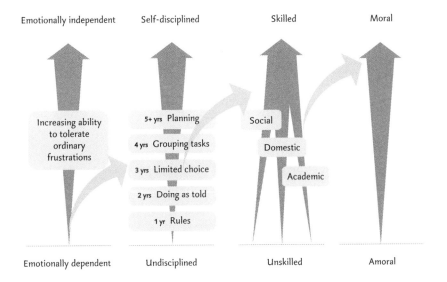

Their developing self-discipline enables them to do the hard work of learning and practising their developing social, domestic and academic skills. As they move along the pathways of becoming more emotionally independent, more self-disciplined and more skilled, their capacity to behave in a moral and ethical way increases.

All this leads to our children becoming adults who are moral, skilled, self-disciplined, and able to tolerate the ordinary frustrations of life and the emotions that come from these frustrations.

So, let's start with supporting their feelings and getting them to do as they are told. This is the foundation. Self-discipline, skills and moral behaviour are bound to follow.

SO WHERE DOES AN EFFECTIVE TIME OUT FIT IN?

The starting place to assist our children on the path to independence begins with our meeting their basic needs for nutrition, safety, comfort and sociability. By supporting our children's feelings and comforting them when they are upset or frustrated, we ensure they are on their way to handling ordinary frustrations and becoming emotionally independent.

Following on from this, we need to teach them to conform to basic rules of the household and the community and to be compliant to simple requests. When we insist our children (tot to teen) do as they are told in response to reasonable requests, we not only take them along the pathway to self-discipline, we also teach them to tolerate the ordinary frustrations of life.

The use of an Effective Time Out may be your simplest way of promoting your tot's, teen's and in-between's journey to adult skills and moral independence.

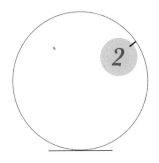

LET'S TAKE TIME
OUT TO DISCUSS
PARENTING TASKS

In order to reach our parenting goals, we need to underpin them
with four main parenting tasks. We need to:

- *support our children's feelings*
- *limit our children's inappropriate behaviour*
- *admire their effort*
- *delight with them in their achievements.*

Most of us put great energy into the first two and regard the latter
two as something we do if and when we remember. I'd like to reverse

that. This book is devoted to *low-energy strategies* for supporting our children's feelings and putting limits on inappropriate behaviour. Hopefully, this avoids our being too exhausted and leaves us with energy to admire our children's effort and delight with them when they achieve.

With our children's feelings being supported and their being less inclined to push boundaries, it means that they can get on with the tasks of developing the social, domestic and academic skills they need to grow to independent adulthood.

Even more importantly, as they increase their ability to cope with the frustrations of life, they have the 'backbone' to develop their values and their virtues and to behave in morally upright ways.

LOW ENERGY? YOU MUST BE JOKING!

'Diane,' I hear you say, 'did you say low-energy strategies? There's nothing low energy about parenting.' As it happens, I agree with you. There is nothing much low energy about parenting. When it comes to all the energy we put into the *services* of parenting — the broken nights, the nappy changing, the food preparation, the school camps, the nightly homework battle, the driving lessons and the broken nights again when we are parenting teens — you are right. There is no such thing as low energy.

However, when it comes to parenting tasks and strategies for supporting our children's feelings, getting them to do as they are told and insisting on the household rules being obeyed, the less energy we put into it and the more energy our children put into it, the better.

SUPPORTING THEIR FEELINGS

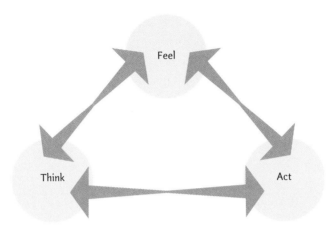

1   How we feel influences how we think and how
    we act (what we do)

2   How we think influences how we feel and how
    we act (what we do)

3   How we act (what we do), influences how we
    feel and how we think

When our children are overwhelmed by feelings of upset or
frustration, they cannot even begin to think of what they should be
doing next to remedy the situation. Until we/they have calmed down
their feelings, they cannot possibly get into 'thinking mode'.

So our first parenting task, when our children are upset, distressed, frustrated or angry, is to help them settle their feelings so that they can get into problem-solving mode, i.e. so they can think about what to do about the situation.

Whether their upset is because the square peg won't go into the round hole, they didn't make the sports team they wanted to, or they cannot find the ball-dress of their dreams, our parenting task is much the same. We support their feelings so that they can tolerate the frustration of the situation and then work out an appropriate action.

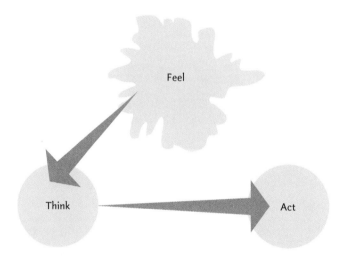

In Chapter Five, we will discuss low-energy ways of settling our children's feelings.

DOING AS TOLD

Our second parenting task is to limit our children's inappropriate behaviour so that they behave in socially appropriate ways and develop self-discipline.

We have lots of nice ways — euphemisms — of saying 'getting our children to do as they are told'. We use expressions like putting in boundaries, setting limits, arranging natural consequences. The less politically correct among us even talk about which punishments work best.

I believe that most parenting battles are fought out over the simple 'doing as told' requests like, 'Hold still while I dress you', 'Leave the baby alone,' 'Don't bounce the ball inside,' 'Make your bed before you go to school,' 'We're leaving the house in ten minutes,' 'I expect to know where you are going and what time you will be home'.

No matter what a parent comes to see me about, sooner or later, it winds up as a compliance issue. If only our children would do as we asked them the first time, there simply wouldn't be a problem.

Most of us put a great deal of effort into getting our children to do as they're told. I favour, instead, low-energy strategies that keep the problem ('I don't want to do that; it looks like I might have to') firmly with our child. How to do that is the major subject of this book.

ADMIRE THEIR EFFORT

At least two generations of parents have put in a lot of mileage trying to promote desirable behaviour through the use of praise. It all started with the early behavioural psychology studies of pigeons and rats, where it was possible to demonstrate that you could get animals to change their behaviour if you rewarded the behaviour that you were trying to encourage. Somehow, these studies got extrapolated from small mammals and birds to human children.

Many of us spent an exhausting time catching our children being good, getting down to their level, using 'I' statements, drawing up star charts and handing out stickers. What a relief to read that Professor Carol Dweck, a psychology professor of Stamford University, says we should stop praising our children for being intelligent and start encouraging them to put effort into cultivating their intelligence. Alfie Kohn, in his wonderful article 'Five Reasons to stop saying Good Job', encourages us to give up on using praise. He cites several studies that show praising children just motivates them to get more praise.

If we want our children to become emotionally mature and handle well the ordinary frustrations of life, to 'try, try and try again', we are far better off admiring their effort and their persistence. Effort and persistence are the hallmark of individuals who are likely to achieve their potential.

It is a worthwhile parenting task and requires very little energy to notice when our children are trying hard and admiring the effort that they put in to things that challenge them and that they find difficult.

For all of us who have sat through long ballet recitals, endless speech competitions, searing-temperature athletics in the middle of the day and freezing afternoons cheering on winter sports — and we have done this for our children whether they have been the prizewinners or the 'also-rans' — admiring their effort is one of the most important tasks of parenthood.

DELIGHT WITH THEM IN THEIR ACHIEVEMENT

I've often pondered just what it is that I am doing when I am alongside my grandchildren saying 'Good boy' or 'Good girl' (and all the variations of these phrases) every time they put in another puzzle piece, add a block to their tower or climb a new piece of playground equipment.

For a long time I felt like a hypocrite. Here I was suggesting that parents should abandon praise and punishment and at the same time I appeared to be lavishing praise for every tiny achievement. Now I see my behaviour differently. I am not trying to use praise as a manipulative device to lead my grandchildren to keep achieving. I am simply delighting with them in the work that they are doing.

This fourth parenting task, being alongside our children and delighting in their achievement, is another one that requires very little effort on our part. The more we notice and support their efforts, the more joy we and they have in whatever they are achieving.

HOW HARD DO I HAVE TO WORK?

Save your energy for the *services* that you give your children.

Learn low-energy strategies to support them when they are unhappy and put boundaries around unacceptable behaviour. That will increase the chances that you have opportunities to admire their efforts and delight in their achievements, because their pleasure and pride in their achievements also gives you pleasure and pride.

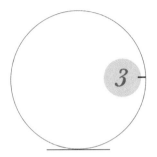

TIME OUT FROM
A VICIOUS CYCLE

We all try to stay away from the 'big scene'. This is the one that finishes with everyone yelling at each other, everyone in tears, everyone in stony silence or each of us with our own variation. Whichever style (angry, upset and/or frosty) we adopt, the outcome is hostility, dislike, alienation and/or distress — not what we had in mind when we held our beautiful newborn baby in our arms.

There are certain things that we predictably do that get us into this pickle. It all starts out with our doing our best to respond to our child when they are angry, upset or non-compliant and somehow it all goes horribly wrong. A wonderfully evocative phrase I learned from my children is 'S/he turned feral'. I am sure that while we parents are experiencing our children turning 'feral', they are experiencing us turning 'feral'. Either way there is that horrible distance between parent and child, which none of us wanted in the first place and now we seem stuck there.

GETTING INTO THE VICIOUS CYCLE

It all starts innocently enough. Our child is upset or frustrated about something, or doesn't feel like doing something we have asked them to, or doesn't feel like stopping doing something we have asked them to stop doing.

Our first attempt to solve the problem is usually some sort of rational explanation. Our child doesn't fancy our explanation and responds with further upset, responds angrily or brushes our attempt aside. Since our first explanation doesn't seem good enough, we attempt to explain it a different way. (Many of us work on the basis, 'If only I can get my explanation just right' — notice how we have taken over the ownership of the problem — 'my child will be ready to respond in a pro-social way.')

Since our explanations don't seem to have done the trick, we may try cajoling our child out of their mood, teasing them into being more cheerful, or jollying them some other way in the vain hope that if we can keep it a positive experience, our child may be more co-operative. No joy there, either.

About this time, we may try to use our powers of persuasion. Either we want them to get over their mood — to see things in a more positive light or, if there is a task to be done, we may try to persuade them of the benefits of the task or the joy of getting it all over as quickly as possible so that they can get on with more exciting things. Still no success.

Our next round may well involve offers or threats of removal, deprivation or consequence or, to use an all-round and increasingly unpopular word, punishment. And, if this is ineffective, we may move on to carrying out the punishment.

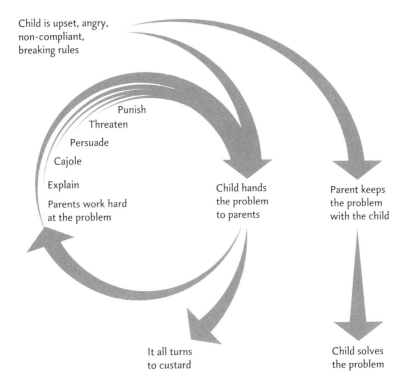

Child is upset, angry, non-compliant, breaking rules

Punish
Threaten
Persuade
Cajole
Explain
Parents work hard at the problem

Child hands the problem to parents

Parent keeps the problem with the child

It all turns to custard

Child solves the problem

Reflect on the scenario

It all began with a child's emotional response or a simple parental request. Now suddenly the atmosphere is hostile, there are two or more very upset people in the room and our relationship with our child appears to have vanished. It has all turned to custard.

Further, if you re-read the previous section, you will see that what started out as the child's problem — they were upset, angry or didn't want to do something — has been neatly handed over and repeatedly handed back to the parent, who has been working very hard to find an appropriate solution. There has to be a better alternative.

OUTCOME OF THIS VICIOUS CYCLE

If we keep getting into these vicious cycles, there are several predictable outcomes.

1   Our child stays incompetent

Instead of our children learning to handle the ordinary frustrations of life, they become increasingly skilled at finding someone else to blame, handing their responsibility to someone else and avoiding difficulties rather than meeting challenges. Instead of our children learning to accept imposed discipline and then moving on to learn how to make wise decisions and to plan, they stay stuck being oppositional. Instead of their developing age-appropriate social, domestic and academic skills, they may find themselves struggling with friendships, not contributing to the household they live in and not achieving their academic potential.

2   As parents we feel incompetent

When our children are melting down over tiny frustrations, when they speak rudely to us, when the simplest parental request turns into an almighty battle, we wonder what we are doing wrong as a parent. We compare ourselves with other parents who seem to have positive relationships with their children and whose children are polite and happily contribute their services to the operation of the family. 'Happily' is probably an exaggeration, but at least the children will do simple things like pack their bags, make their beds and remember where they left their shoes.

We feel helpless and incompetent as a parent and wonder where we went so horribly wrong.

3   The penalty is distance

With enough of these nasty scenarios happening we wonder about our connection to our child. We love them to bits but we don't like their company. We set out to enjoy our parenting and find ourselves fantasising about boarding schools in distant places for four-year-olds. And, above all, we find these negative thoughts about our children and the wish to have some distance from them very, very painful.

AVOIDING THE VICIOUS CYCLE

I can't promise you that your child will never again get angry or upset, won't challenge you on a simple parenting request or will never swear again. All these behaviours are bound to happen, but we can choose a different way of responding to them.

Instead of hooking into cajoling, persuading, threatening and punishing, we are far better off not taking the problem on ourselves, but finding a way to keep the problem with our children. If they can become good problem solvers, they are on their way to becoming pleasant and independent children and young adults.

Choosing a virtuous pathway

When our children are sad or angry, we need to find a way to support them while they settle their feelings. Once their feelings are settled, they will be able to get into problem-solving mode. They may even be ready to ask for some advice!

When our children are reluctant to respond to simple, reasonable parenting requests or are determined to hit, taunt, tease, swear or bully, they need us to disengage from them so that they have only their own resistance to struggle with.

Whichever pathway we choose — to support our child's feelings or to distance ourselves from their unreasonable behaviour — we are keeping an age-appropriate problem with our child and providing an appropriate atmosphere for them to grapple with solutions. The details of 'how to' are the subject of the rest of this book.

Outcome of good parenting choices

Whether we are supporting their feelings or putting boundaries around and limits on inappropriate behaviour, the outcomes of our repeatedly getting it right are predictable.

1 Our child becomes more competent

As our children tolerate the ordinary frustrations of growing up, they become competent at handling social relationships, learning new and more difficult skills and making the best of their educational opportunities.

As our children learn to overcome their own resistance and do as they are told to reasonable requests, as they learn to control what comes out of their mouths and what their hands and feet are doing to others, they become increasingly self-disciplined. As they learn to make good choices and learn the skills of short-term and long-term planning, they become increasingly competent and much more pleasant to be with.

2 As parents we feel competent

When our children are behaving appropriately, when we are proud to be in their company, when we rejoice at their increasing competence, we also know that we are getting it right as parents. Instead of wondering what on earth they are going to do next, we feel confident and competent in our parenting and find parenting less burdensome and more rewarding.

3 The reward is closeness

With our children behaving appropriately and developing their own personalities and character, we will find ourselves feeling closer to them. We are free to enjoy their company and feel proud to be with them. We look forward to seeing them and miss them when they are not there.

And that is the sales pitch for this book.

If we can stay out of the vicious cycle and instead make an appropriate choice of support or limit, we can be confident that we can watch our children's growth and development with delight, that we will know how to handle the inevitable parenting bumps in the road, and that together we will weather the inevitable tough stuff that families face.

With a combination of support and limits we can enjoy our children's company and the privileged experience of being a parent.

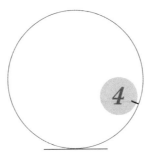

TIME OUT FROM WHAT?
PART ONE OF
MY LEARNING

Before we can begin to talk about Time Out, we need to know 'Time Out from what?' The short answer is 'Time Out from our support and services'. All said in one brief phrase. It seems so obvious now. But my journey to get there happened over a five-year period and I would like to share that journey with you.

THE GOOD OLD DAYS

Most of us who are old enough now to be the grandparents of young grandchildren (OK, time to confess, my generation is already or soon will be turning 60) were raised by parents who didn't hesitate to use some sort of punishment for their children's wrongdoing. We children took it for granted that if we had done something wrong, a punishment would follow. It felt right and mostly it felt fair and, more often than not, we learned not to repeat that behaviour. Some of us learned fast and some of us had to get the same punishment several times before we got the message.

PSYCHOLOGY 101

Then along came B.F. Skinner and his generation of behavioural psychologists. Not only did they show that punishment worked but they also showed that rats and pigeons responded well to some sort of reward for getting a right answer. When I was at Auckland University, I spent a considerable portion of my third year (1967) training a rat to tell the difference between horizontal and vertical lines. The reward for the right decision was a food pellet. The punishment for the wrong decision involved a short drop into a net.

This concept of reward and punishment, positive reinforcement and negative reinforcement was translated, experimentally proven and transferred into ways of changing human behaviour. Thus parents and teachers took up the banner of 'catch them being good' and an endless round of stickers, star charts and prolific praise began. At the same time, the word 'punishment' fell out of favour and we all began searching for the natural and logical consequences that would teach our children the error of their ways.

When I became a Family Therapist, I spent a lot of my time

teaching parents the seven things that they had to do to praise effectively and introducing them to a 'new and better' punishment. It was called Time Out and I was able to teach them how to stop smacking and start to use something more repeatable and effective.

THE YEQUANA INDIANS

In 1989, I read a book that changed my thinking. The author, Jean Liedloff, lived among a tribe known as the Yequana Indians who lived off a tributary of the Orinoco River in the highlands of Venezuela. They were a gentle people who had babies who never cried and children who were extremely obedient. A parent only had to ask them to do something and they would scurry off to do it and be pleased to be asked to contribute. Equally intriguing, the parent only had to express displeasure — what we would call a mild growl — and the child would do their level best to correct their error.

How did they do that? I read and reread Jean Liedloff's book *The Continuum Concept* searching for understanding and then wondering what on earth it might have to do with an urban Kiwi parent and child.

Meeting the babies' needs

Yequana mothers have no concept of babies being needy or demanding. They carry their babies all the time and feed them when they indicate they are hungry. So no baby ever needs to cry from hunger or loneliness. Most of the time, their in-arm babies sleep or are passive observers of what is going on. Because they are never shut away from busy village life, there is always something to watch when they are awake. So no baby ever needs to cry from boredom and no Yequana ever has to worry about entertaining their baby.

Now I understood why the in-arms babies never cried. What about the toddlers?

Unconditional support

The Yequana secret seems to lie in their unconditional support — without words — when their children are upset or distressed. If a crawler or toddler — in fact, a child of any age — runs to their mother mildly upset or in distress, the Yequana mum scoops them up into her arms and carries on with whatever it was she had previously been doing. No 'What's the matter?', 'Who upset you?', 'What's all this fuss about?' — just wordless comfort. It all seemed very strange to me, who believed that as a mother I was there to sort out my children's problems and make them feel better.

I began to ponder on the idea of leaving our children to get on with their own learning and only to comfort when they came to us upset. Having a five-year-old of my own presented me with an opportunity.

My opportunity

One day Deb was playing next door with Gemma, who was an equally lovely little five-year-old. I was enjoying the three-minute respite you get when your child is playing happily next door when suddenly, Deb burst in crying, 'Gemma was *mean* to me!'. It seemed the perfect opportunity to 'make like a Yequana mother'.

I put my arm around my daughter, failed entirely to be silent and muttered, 'Sweetheart, how awful for you' . . . and waited . . . and waited.

Since my usual response would have been wordy and inter-ventionist, Deborah looked up at me with a bewildered expression as if to say 'Are you my mother? You look like her, but you don't sound like my mother.' Meanwhile my internal voice was questioning, 'Well, this might work in the highlands of Venezuela but it appears to have very little application in Auckland, New Zealand.'

Since neither of us could work out what to do, we held still, frozen in this position for at least fifteen seconds. It felt a great deal longer. Deb announced, 'Bye, Mum', and raced back next door to play with Gemma. I sat there stunned.

Clearly something different and significant had just happened. Deborah ran in upset. I had given her five words of empathy and a wordless hug and she ran off happily, with her problem apparently solved.

I knew it was important. I knew it meant something significant. But what exactly did it mean?

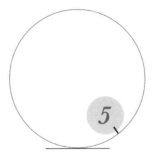

TIME OUT FROM BLAMING, CRITICISING AND LECTURING

I began to reflect on what I would normally do when Deb would rush in upset.

BLAME

It is a feature of our Kiwi upbringing to believe in fair play — we are always willing to believe there is another side to every story. Given this, our first response to our child's being upset by another child is often, 'So, what did you do to Gemma?'

Often our first impulse is to seek to place blame and, more often than not, we try to place the blame on our child. Instead of feeling heard and comforted, our child could be forgiven for thinking that we care more about the plight of the other child than we do about them.

CRITICISM

A criticism tends to start with 'Why can't you just . . . ?' Sometimes we say it out loud; sometimes we just think it. 'Why can't you just play nicely together?' However, a question — particularly a rhetorical question — beginning with 'Why can't you just . . .', implies that our children's feelings are not important — that they should simply get over it. We are implying that our children shouldn't have these feelings of sadness or anger or frustration.

Criticism tends to wound all children, particularly our sensitive ones. To imply criticism just for having feelings is unfair and unhelpful.

DISTRACTION

Another way in which we dismiss our children's feelings is by trying to distract them from having the feelings. Although in the short term this may avoid a tantrum or stop our children from being upset, it takes away their experience of having their feelings, experiencing the feelings and then, within the safety of parental support/cuddle/listening, being able to cope with the feelings and move on. In other words, if we are distracting our children from having feelings, we are not only invalidating their feelings, we are sending them the wrong message about actually having feelings.

When a small child comes to us upset we often try terribly hard to get their mind onto something else. We may even insist that they don't think about or talk about whatever is bothering them. In the context of Deborah and Gemma's spat, distraction would look like: 'Well, don't worry, darling, I am sure Gemma didn't mean to upset you. Let's not think about that. Shall we read a book together?'

Many of us start with our young babies. If they are upset we quickly look for something interesting, noisy or diverting to make them feel better. If the first thing doesn't work, we try something else, and if that doesn't work we try something else.

Please don't misunderstand me. A little bit of light distraction goes a long way. However, if it isn't going to work easily it probably isn't going to work at all, so we should avoid working terribly hard at it. Also, if distraction is your favourite method of getting your child to do as she is told, you are probably working hard at your child's compliance and she is not working at it at all.

EXPLANATIONS

My first job was as a teacher so it won't surprise you that, if blaming, criticising and distracting hadn't worked, my next tactic was always to launch into an explanation.

'Don't be upset, darling. Maybe you touched some of Gemma's toys that are precious to her.' Or 'Maybe Gemma is just having a bad day.' Or — a fatal error, guaranteed to gets howls of protests out of any self-respecting youngster — 'Maybe you're tired. Remember last night when you mucked about at bedtime?'

When our children are upset, explaining to them the 'enemy's' position or pointing out their own contribution to the problem is likely to result in the child yelling back, 'You never listen' or 'You always take her side' or 'I'm not tired'.

MINI-LECTURES

The first time I heard the term 'mini-lecture' was when I heard Barbara Coloroso (author of *Kids Are Worth It*) speak.

A mini-lecture is a collection of ideas or a small homily we have trotted out so frequently and with such consistency that, after the first five words, our child can finish the speech.

In our household, mini-lecture Number 43, saved specially for occasions such as these, would be: 'You don't know how lucky you are to have a little girl next door to play with. When I was your age, I would have given anything to have . . .' And so on.

Most of us have many favourite mini-lectures derived from our own experience that we assume will also apply to our children's experience. Not surprisingly, our children neither learn from them nor are comforted by them. More likely they'll interrupt with 'Yeah, yeah, I know. When you were my age . . .'

PROBLEM SOLVING

We may try this first or leave it till last. Either way it is doomed.

> **Mum**: How about you go and ride your bikes
> together?
> **Child**: Naa.
> **Mum** (*revving up the enthusiasm*): Well, how about you
> put on your Jellybean make-up together?
> **Child**: Naa-aa.
> **Mum** (*very brightly and with great enthusiasm*): I know!
> How about you ring up Gemma and she can
> come over here? Remember that wonderful
> jigsaw Grandma gave you last week? Gemma

could come over and you both could do it together.

Child: Naa-aa-aa.

Mum (*exhausted and exasperated*): Well, why don't you just go to your room and sulk?

What is wrong with this picture? This began as a small problem between two five-year-olds, and here I am working like crazy to come up with solutions. My daughter is standing there quite relaxed, not taking any part in the solution, just saying 'Naa-aa' every now and again to keep me out of her face or to keep me working hard at *her* problem.

A LIST OF DON'TS

All I had done was offer her a comforting arm and some words of support and she seemed to be able to settle her feelings and think about what to do next. As I reflected on that, I thought about all the things that I would normally do — and they became my 'list of don'ts'.

1　Don't blame

2　Don't criticise

3　Don't distract

4　Don't explain

5　Don't give mini-lectures

6　Don't problem solve.

Notice that this looks very similar to the list of actions in the vicious cycle we described in relation to non-compliance.

WHAT ELSE IS THERE?

So if we are going to give up on blaming, criticising, distracting, explaining, mini-lecturing and problem solving, what is there left for a parent to do when confronted with an upset or angry child?

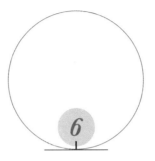

BORING
CUDDLES
FOR ALL AGES

Putting an arm round my upset five-year-old, muttering 'how awful for you' and waiting till she moved away had worked so simply. Was it a one-off fluke or was it the germ of a strategy? It turned out to be a useful strategy that I have taught individually to clients and through my seminars, articles and books. I am often stopped in supermarkets and told, 'Your Boring Cuddles work so well.'

A few days ago the same Deb — now 22 — came home with a story about her little niece, my granddaughter, now two and a half. Dani is a very fiery and very sensitive little girl. Deb has grown up listening to me talk about my parenting strategies (often being the first guinea pig of some new hare-brained idea I have hatched!) and is familiar with the concept of the Boring Cuddle. She shared this story with me.

Aunty Deb was picking her niece, Dani, up from day-care. Dani was busy preparing play-dough delights in the toy kitchen. She was extremely reluctant to stop 'cooking' and leave the play-dough behind, but it was time to go home. Deb suggested she put the play-dough in the toy fridge, which Dani did, but when she scooped her up to go, Dani burst into tears. Deb cuddled her on her shoulder and the dialogue went something like this.

Dani (*very upset*): Pla-a-y-dough!

Deb (*gently*): O-h-h-h-h Dani.

Dani (*more upset*): Pla-a-y-dough!!!!

Deb: You really wanted to play with the play-dough, didn't you darling?

Dani (*miserably*): Yes!!!

Deb: And you're really not ready to come home yet.

Dani (*sniffing and very miserable*): No!

Deb: You wanted to play with the play-dough.

Dani (*small sob*): Yes . . .

Deb: Even though you know we are going to have lots of fun at home?

Dani: Yes.

Deb then cuddled Dani all the way to the car and put her in her car-seat. Deb handed Dani a little toy.

Deb: Would you like to look after this on the way home, Dani?

Dani: Yes . . . Debu? (her name for Deb)

Deb: Yes, Dani?

Dani: Sad . . . getting better (*small smile*).

THREE ELEMENTS

Whether our children are eighteen months or eighteen years old, there are three elements to supporting their feelings that seem to be really effective:

1   Put their feelings into words

2   Stick with them

3   Wait till *they* are finished and ready to move on.

Put their feelings into words

For our babies and crawlers who are pre-verbal, and our older children who need to know that we understand how distressed they are, putting their feelings into words is a powerful and supportive way of letting them know we really care.

Never, *ever* say, 'I know how you feel.' It just invites, 'No you don't' or 'Prove it'.

The best way to show your child that you fully understand how awful their situation is is to use empathy. Put into words — as precisely as possible — what is bothering them.

- *'You are so upset about that.'*
- *'That really hurts.'*
- *'You hate leaving your friend's place.'*
- *'That other team was really hard to play against.'*
- *'I know how much you wanted to go there and I am so sorry it didn't work out.'*
- *'It is really hard to get bad marks when you have worked so hard.'*
- *'It is really hard to get bad marks.' (tactfully biting your tongue hard to stop yourself from saying '. . . even if you know you haven't done the work')*

- *'I am so-o-o sorry you've been let down by her again.'*

If you cannot think of anything to say, an empathetic 'O-h-h-h-h-h' will cover almost any topic.

Stick with them

In the example of Deb and Dani, you can see that Deb stuck with Dani's feelings until she had expressed everything she needed to. When our older children begin to tell us a story of upset for them, the great temptation is to pick up on the first few phrases and launch into problem solving. Instead, our child or teen will feel far better heard if we stay with the story, keep asking versions of 'And what happened next?' and keep very focused on our child's experience.

Some children like to talk, some children like to grunt a monosyllable. 'How was your day?' may get you a five-minute diatribe or a single 'Yuk!' Either way, our job is to receive the information our child wishes to give us and be prepared to accept just that. Whatever their response, linger just a little longer to show that you are not impatient to get away from them.

Waiting till they are ready to move on: the Boring Cuddle

The term Boring Cuddle has two parts. The term 'Boring' means that you do not give any input, confining yourself to mutters or phrases of support. It is a very kind way of instructing you as the parent not to blame, criticise, distract, explain, mini-lecture or problem solve.

With a little child, a Boring Cuddle may literally be a wordless cuddle in a parent's arms. With an older child, it may be an arm around their shoulder. With a teen, it may be the fact that you are sitting there with a full cup of coffee in your hand, i.e. you are probably there for at least ten minutes. The car is built for Boring Cuddles. You are strapped in together and, since the car is moving at speed, no one is going anywhere and you are available to be fully present.

The term Boring Cuddle also means that you are going to stay fully present until your child is ready to move on. Whether it is to go out and play, to lapse into comfortable silence or to move on to another topic, a Boring Cuddle finishes when your child's emotional tank has refilled and he is ready to face the rest of his day.

What about advice?

'But surely,' I hear you say, 'I am entitled to give some advice. All those years of experience have to be worth something.' You are quite correct. All these years of experience are worth a great deal, but trying to impose your ideas on an upset or unwilling child or teen is bound to end horribly.

If we have been listening with empathy and allowing our children to give full vent to their feelings, we just may be graced with the magic words, 'What do you think I should do?' Congratulations! That privilege has been hard-won. To get to this point, you have had to develop sufficient restraint that your child trusts that your advice will not include criticism or lectures.

Deliver your advice in a way that your child understands that you are sharing *your* ideas and he is free to use them only if they are useful to his circumstances.

What if I have a great idea?

What happens if we, as parents, have this great solution and our child has not asked our opinion? Is there a way to give advice without their experiencing it as us problem solving and therefore to be rejected? The best way that I have found, if I have an idea burning to be shared but I am not sure how receptive my child is, is to say, 'I have an idea of what may help. Do you want to hear it?'

More often than not this is met with a shouted 'No!' It is easy to get offended at this point and to start berating our child for his rudeness. If you can muster the self-restraint, an elegant response to a yelled 'No!' is to say evenly and quietly, 'That's fine. If you want to know at any stage, come back and I'll make a point of remembering.'

It is amazing how often, somewhere between ten and 30 minutes later, I have had a child return — as if it is their initiative — saying, 'Mum! About that idea you had . . . what was it?'

WHY ALL THIS BOTHER
ABOUT EMOTIONAL SUPPORT?

If we are to use Time Out effectively, it has to be Time Out *from* something.

If we build a culture where our children's upsets are met with blame, criticism, distraction and lectures — all of which often finish in a shouting match — they are scarcely going to notice when we are cross.

If we build a climate with our children of readily available Emotional Support for when they are upset, if we support their feelings and listen to their woes, they will notice when we are outraged or when we withdraw support and be far more likely to develop the self-restraint that leads to mature young adulthood.

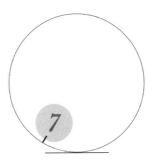

WHY CHILDREN SHOULD DO AS THEY ARE TOLD

Wouldn't it be wonderful if children did what we asked them to the first time? Or even did things without being asked? How many times, from six months to six years, do you think you will have asked your children to let you dress them or to go and get dressed? How many times from six to sixteen do you imagine you will be saying, 'Go and do your homework'? Wouldn't it be great if our children did as they were told? Think of the time and energy we would save.

LET'S HEAR IT FOR
TOLERATING FRUSTRATION

In order for our children to be compliant, they have to tolerate the frustration of doing something they would rather not do. Maybe they would rather not do it at all or maybe they would rather do it when they have finished watching the next DVD. Whatever it is, they certainly don't want to do it right away.

In overcoming their resistance to complying with an ordinary request, our children are learning to tolerate the ordinary frustrations of life. By becoming obedient to simple parental requests, they are not only on the path to becoming self-disciplined, they are also on the pathway to becoming emotionally mature. It is the mark of an emotionally mature person that they can make themselves do the things that they would rather not do but know are necessary.

By insisting that our children do as they are told to simple requests, we are helping them to become mature, independent young adults.

LET'S HEAR IT FOR SOCIALISATION

As human beings, we are social creatures, and most of us feel the innate need to be part of a social group. Originally, we lived in tribes and were mutually dependent on each other. Later on, we lived in villages and were both dependent on and accountable to each other. Our families were larger and more intergenerational than today's and so issues of compliance were learned through observation of older children and were enforced by all responsible adults of the social grouping.

Today, where a family group may be as small as one parent and one child, we are on our own as we try to socialise our children, and many of us feel as if it is 'us against our child' when it comes to simple requests.

IT IS HARDER THAN IT USED TO BE

When our grandparents told their children to put on their socks, it was highly likely that the children complied without question. Of course there is the possibility that the previous generation of children was far less assertive than today's, lacked in initiative and courage, had less imagination or were simply meek and mild. Unlikely!

I think the reason that previous generations of children would comply readily with a simple parental request was because when a parent said, 'Put on your socks', they had the backing of almost every adult in any position of authority in that society. The family members agreed, the headmaster agreed, the police agreed, the church agreed and the government agreed.

Today, when we ask our children to put their socks on (or any other simple parental request) we have a sense of a whole lot of 'thought police', politically correct people bleating, 'But surely it is *their* feet. If they go outside and their feet are cold, they will learn not to do it next time. If their feet hurt, they will surely change their minds. What about the child's thoughts and feelings?'

I feel like shouting, 'Where are you when my child gets a cold three days from now and I have to go to work? The only person who learns from that experience is the parent. Don't you understand that children only get flu on weekdays? If they get splinters in their feet, who do you think is going to have to get them out? If they get their feet cut, who do you think is going to have to take them to A and E?'

And apart from that, while I think that it is excellent for children to develop critical thinking skills, debating skills, initiative, courage and assertiveness, the suitable place to practise these is not over simple, parenting requests.

OUR CHILDREN NEED TO FIT IN

We need our children to learn compliance to simple and reasonable requests, so that they can fit into larger social groups when and as they encounter them. It is our job as parents to teach them to do so. It is much harder to do that in the sort of isolation in which small families live, so what is a parent to do?

In today's environment, since much of our parenting is done in unsupported isolation, most of us don't have the live-in daily back-up of extended family, and very few of us belong to a village where every adult feels a responsibility and a connection to every child, we are simply going to have to be more skilled in how we go about raising our children to independent adulthood.

Since it is such hard work teaching our children to be compliant, it is important to remind ourselves why we are working so hard. Let's think about our parenting objectives when it comes to compliance.

When we ask a child to do something we have short-term, medium-term and long-term objectives.

Short-term objective

We may only be aware at the time of the short-term objective, which is to get something done. Usually it is some simple and often-repeated task:

- *Hold still while I change your nappy.*
- *Let's get you dressed, please.*
- *Do up your seat-belt, please.*
- *Go and get your homework, please.*
- *I need to know where you are going and when you will be home.*
- *Pack your bag for tomorrow, please.*

Let's deal with 'please' right now. 'Please' shouldn't make the least difference to whether or not your child carries out the request, but you are modelling (the most effective way to teach a child) good manners and that can never go amiss. Of course you need to be prepared for the fact that no matter how impeccable your manners, your child may not necessarily do what you have asked her to do.

In every person's day, child or adult, there are hundreds of tiny tasks that need to be done. When I was a child we were often quoted 'A stitch in time saves nine'. Also quoted at us was Benjamin Franklin's saying: 'For the want of a nail, the shoe was lost; for the want of a shoe, the horse was lost; and for the want of a horse, the rider was lost, being overtaken and slain by the enemy, all for the want of care about a horseshoe nail.'

At the time I always thought, 'Boring, boring, b-o-o-o-ring.' Unfortunately, the practice of 'Do it now and do it quickly' for the small tasks of life does seem to be the most efficient, and for our children to learn to do as they are told over the tiny tasks makes life much more pleasant.

Sweat the small stuff

Parents who are struggling with their children's behaviour often quote to me the title of Richard Carlson's book, *Don't Sweat the Small Stuff*. They feel that they should deal with the truly awful behaviour and not worry about simple compliance to tiny tasks. I couldn't *disagree* more.

Our parenting days are made up of lots of tiny 'small stuff' requests like the ones listed. Two things to think about:

> *1*   Think about how many times you will change your child's nappy from six months to when they're toilet-trained. Think about how many times your baby to young adult will need to get dressed. Think about how many times a school bag will need to be unpacked or packed. Do you really want to battle this each time or do you want to get it sorted out once and for all?

2   It doesn't matter what it is about (nappies, dressing, school bags, etc), it all boils down to complying with simple requests.

'Sweating the small stuff' *is* the big stuff.

Medium-term objective

If your child spends a lot of energy resisting simple requests, she is using up the time and energy she could better use for learning new skills that are useful to her rather than refining an old skill — resisting compliance — that is ultimately bad for her.

If she has already resisted getting up, having a nappy change, getting dressed, sitting down for breakfast and having her teeth cleaned and it is only 7.45am, what sort of a day do you think you are in for?

If she has already resisted getting up, getting dressed, packing her bag, making her bed, and getting out the door in time, what sort of a child do you think you are sending to school? A child who is ready to benefit from the wisdom and experience of the classroom teacher, or a child who is ready to resist a new set of requests, such as 'Take out your books', 'Find your pencil', 'Stop hitting Jason', 'Start writing'?

So our medium-term objective is to have our children do as they are told.

Long-term objective

A child who is extremely non-compliant eventually begins to sabotage the relationships in her life. Her parents may be endlessly forgiving but exhausted, her teacher looks forward to weekends and her friends are likely to get sick of her too.

When families approach me worried about their child's progress at school or lack of friends, the first question I am likely to ask is, 'What is her compliance like?' If the response is something like, 'Well, she is very strong-willed', I am likely to recommend that we look first at her compliance at home. If we can improve this, it is amazing how often it flows on to school and social situations.

If we get improvements at home but not at school, we are in a strong position to go to the school and say, 'We have achieved these changes at home. Can we now look at how these strategies might work in the school context?'

A child who learns compliance at home will not only have better relationships with parents, teachers and friends, but is also on the road to becoming a self-disciplined adult. This is our long-term objective. If we accept that we are on a continuum of development from an undisciplined baby to a self-disciplined adult, then each step needs to be made before our children are ready to move on to the next.

Unless our children pass through the 'Doing as told' phase they are going to have trouble handling limited choice and grouping tasks together, and as they get older they are going to have trouble looking ahead at the consequences of their action or inaction.

Parents of teen-aged children often ask me, 'Is it too late?' My response is unconditionally, 'Never.' If I thought it was ever too late, why would I work with the parents of children over the age of eleven?

RESPECT — OURS AND THEIRS

Whatever age, we need to claim *our* self-respect so that when we make a simple request, we expect it to be done. Whatever age the children we are raising are, we need to respect *their* ability to comply with our simple requests. Whatever their age, we need to keep our eye to their future. Children who comply with simple parental requests are on the pathway to becoming self-disciplined adults.

WE WILL LIKE THEM A WHOLE LOT BETTER

One of the toughest parenting moments most of us will go through at some time or another is when we do not like our children. This is separate from loving them. Of course we love them. Even when we are going through our blackest moments of 'I do not like you. You are behaving horribly. I'm not even sure that I want to be in the same room as you. I wonder if there is a boarding school for four-year-olds a couple of hundred kilometres away', we keep on clothing and feeding and educating and guarding their safety and rapidly forgiving them. That's parental love.

'Liking them' is another matter. If they fight you every step of the way, if they are rude, cheeky and non-compliant, if you are in a patch of waking in the morning with a sinking feeling of 'Oh no! Not you again!', then it is time to do something about their compliance.

If our children are reasonably compliant, we can enjoy their company. If we enjoy their company, we will want to spend time with them. That is one of the best reasons I can think of for teaching our children to do as they are told.

That's the end of the sales pitch for compliance. How do we get it?

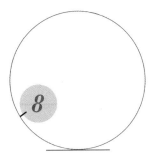

ASK AND TELL

About 80 per cent of all our compliance problems would be solved if we could be confident that we are entitled to ask our child to comply. If we ask with conviction, recognise when they have said 'No' to a simple request and then follow up by telling them clearly and firmly what we expect, we often do not have to deal with 'What on earth are we going to do next?'

ASKING

Often our rows with our children begin with a simple request.
- *Hold still while I change you.*
- *Leave the cat lying in the sun.*
- *It is time to clean your teeth.*
- *Get your gear off the table and set it, please.*
- *Please write down the name, address and phone number of where you are going.*

They do it

One possibility is that our child does as they have been asked. That is actually what we are after and it is important, if it doesn't happen, to remember that was what we had in mind.

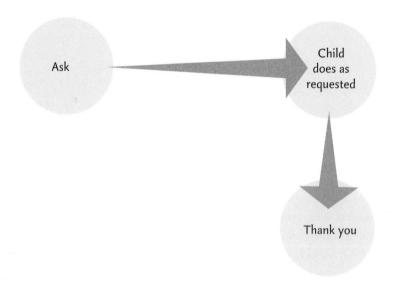

Ways of asking

There seems to be a lot of advice about the correct way to ask. It is easy to infer from these ideas that, if *you* don't ask the right way, then it is quite understandable that your child feels entitled not to do as asked. I do not agree with this.

As far as I am concerned, a child should respond to small, reasonable parental requests by doing them. End of story.

You may appreciate a small example from home. First time around, I tended to express myself gently. 'I'd rather you didn't do that.' My children are smart so, after the whole thing had escalated into my yelling, 'How many times do I have to tell you not to do that!' they would often try sidetracking me with, 'Well, you could have just told me straight out.' My response was always, 'How long have you lived with me? You knew exactly what I meant. Don't try that one on me.'

The seduction of electronics

I am often asked, 'But what if they are watching TV?'

As you would with any adult, the normal rules of courtesy apply. If a child is mid-programme (which you have deliberately or inadvertently permitted) it is probably not fair to expect them to stop what they are doing and willingly race off to do as asked. It would be far more graceful (and productive) to wait for the next ad-break.

Somehow, this response always leads to the next question, 'But what if it is a DVD and there is no ad-break?' or 'What if it is the Cartoon Network?'

It all goes back to our planning and responsibility. Before we allow our children to sit in front of some electronic device that is programmed to be seductive, compelling and suck our children's brains into the screen, it would be a good idea to check whether there are tasks that need to be done before our children become unavailable.

'You need to be dressed, teeth cleaned and bag packed and then you are free to watch your DVD' is so much more likely to be successful than, 'After your programme is finished, you will brush your teeth and pack you bag, won't you?'

If you must make a request of your child (and this applies to adults as well) while they are electronically involved (this applies to computers, games and cellphones as well), make sure that they have come to a stopping point, 'pushed pause', turned away from the device or turned it off and are willing to give you their full attention. Otherwise, you are fighting uphill, unlikely to gain compliance and likely to wind up in a 'Just wait till I've finished; I've been unreasonably interrupted' row.

Ask and observe

Now let's look at the options (other than our child does as asked) once we have made a request for them to do something or to stop doing something.

Let's say we make the request from whatever place we are doing things: 'Please pick up the blocks and put them in the block box.' (Depending on our child's age, it could just as easily be 'Hold still while I put your shoes on you', 'Please set the table', 'It's time you were doing your homework', or myriad other small requests we may make in any normal parenting day.)

There are many ways in which our child might respond:
- *'It's too hard'*
- *'Why do you always pick on me?'*
- *'I don't want to'*
- *'Will you help me?'*
- *'I'm not going to'*
- *A blank stare*
- *Totally ignoring what we've asked*
- *'Yes, Mummy' (while doing absolutely nothing about it)*
- *'Yes, Mummy' (and wandering off in the general direction but never getting there)*

No matter which way the response goes — other than doing as requested — our child has just delivered one or other of the three varieties of 'No'.

THREE VARIETIES OF 'NO'

Anything other than complying with a request is a variety of 'No'. Barbara Colorosa describes the three varieties of 'No' as Sad, Mad and Distancing.

1   The 'Sad' responses are the many variations of 'It's too hard', 'I'm too tired', 'My feet hurt too much', 'I c-a-a-a-a-n't', 'It's not fair', 'There's too many' or 'Why me?' — often uttered in a prolonged wail or ear-grating whine.

2   The 'Mad' responses are the many variations of 'It's not my turn', 'I won't', 'You're not the boss of me', 'You can't make me', uttered in an angry and accusing tone of voice.

3   The 'Distancing' responses are not quite so 'in your face'. Your child may smile endearingly, even agree to do as you have asked — and then apparently vanish into thin air. He may look at you with a totally blank and uncomprehending expression. He may say 'In a minute', but apparently this minute has thousands more seconds than the conventional 60. He may not even glance up at you but carry on with whatever he was doing.

These three responses (Sad, Mad or Distancing) — or an outright 'No' — are ways our children have of letting us know that they have little intention of doing as we have asked them to.

Many parents who come to see me have already had their child's hearing tested. They have assumed that their child's unwillingness to listen and respond might be an inability to hear. They have been 'sucked in' by a child whose variety of 'No' is to quietly ignore his parents' requests.

The tempting vicious cycle

Beware being seduced into a vicious cycle. Because we cannot quite imagine that our child has had the cheek to decide that they don't have to take any notice of our request, we often get seduced into thinking that we haven't quite asked the right way.

We get sucked into explaining, persuading, cajoling and threatening on the basis that 'If only I can say it just the right way, my child will be sure to comply'.

You've just been told 'No'.

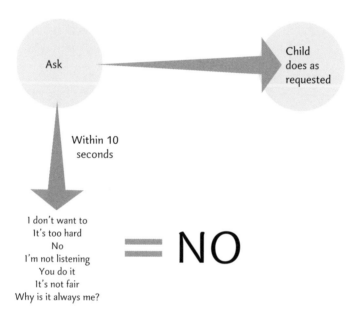

By your child not moving to do as he has been told, he has just indicated a big, resounding 'NO'. No — I don't intend to stop what I am doing. No — I do not have to do as you have asked me. No — no amount of persuading, cajoling, explaining or pleading is going to make the least difference. NO NO NO NO NO!

If you have asked once and there is no activity in the direction of compliance, whether it is through the child getting incompetent, helpless and sad or angry, shouting and blustering or running away, or ignoring or grinning but not doing, your child has just said 'No.'

Time is running out

Your child makes up his mind in less than ten seconds whether he is going to do as asked or not. If, after he had made his decision, you keep on nagging, persuading, debating or pleading, you are merely weakening your position.

Imagine an old-fashioned egg-timer. Once you have made a request, the 'sands' of your power start running out and guess who they are running into? After you have asked your child to do something and he has decided 'No', your power starts running out and your child's power begins increasing.

Your
power

Your
child's
power

Move now

The sooner you move right next to your child, the sooner you begin to gain some power. You've already found out that your child is not taking any notice of you from a distance. No amount of shouting and threatening is going to make your child take notice of you. Going right over to him will.

This is the single most important piece of advice, in relation to gaining your child's compliance, that I can give you. It is deceptively simple, and yet we all find it harder to do than thinking we can stay put and raise the volume. Stop what you are doing (or get out of your chair) and go over right next to your child. You are cranking it up to TELL your child what you expect.

TELL POWERFULLY

Once you are standing right next to your child, repeat the request quietly and determinedly.

- *I've asked you pick up the blocks.*
- *I've asked you to get dressed.*
- *I've asked you to leave the cat alone.*
- *I've asked you to come and give me a hand with the dishes.*
- *I've asked you to get ready to leave the house.*

There are several elements to telling powerfully that will make your request more effective: space invade, height advantage, strong 'optic nerve' contact and a quietly controlled voice.

Space invade

I cannot emphasise often enough how important it is to go over and stand next to your child. Strangely enough, many of us do not seem to realise that calling, shouting, threatening, explaining and even screaming are mostly ineffective. Our children seem to have a message loop running in their brain — no doubt as a result of experience — that repeats to them, 'While Mum's or Dad's mouth is doing overtime at full volume and from a distance, I am still safe and

I don't have to do anything.'

Once they *experience* us (I use that word rather than 'see' because even the child who doesn't look up experiences us coming into their space) advancing, they are likely to be on full alert and ready, however unwillingly, to hear what we have to say.

With a parent standing right next to them, it is impossible for them to keep on tuning out. This is also a wonderful strategy for teens who persist in speaking on the phone, staying focused on the computer screen or even texting while you are unsuccessfully trying to engage them. Try going right up next to them. If you want to be extra polite, try saying, 'When you have finished', but stay put right next to them. You have just demonstrated the power of proximity.

Height advantage

From days of yore, the monarchy has always ruled from a throne. Furthermore, the throne is usually on a high plinth. Instinctively, we accept edicts from taller people.

When you approach your child to tell them what you want, stand tall. It is easier to do this when they are much shorter than you and it is easier to do this when they are sitting down. That is why it is better to establish the authority of 'Parent Power' when they are little.

Should you be reading this at a time when your child is already taller than you, think power and think tall and it will have a very similar effect.

You will read and see lots of advice about 'getting down to their level'. I think this is just the right thing to do when you are offering comfort and just the wrong thing to do when you are wishing to project authority. Frankly, if you are crouching down next to an angry child, you are inviting a push on the shoulder or a poke in the eye. Stand tall.

'Optic nerve' contact

Look directly at them. If their eyes are not available, glare at where their eyes would be if they were looking you in the eye. Don't get into a row over 'Look at me while I am talking to you'. A row over eye contact simply means that you have two rows on the go — 'Look at me' and whatever your original request was.

Think of yourself as targeting their optic nerves. Because you are a parent, you have the capacity to access their optic nerves through their skull. It doesn't matter if you are presented with the top of your child's head, the side of their head or the back of their head, make sure your eyes are drilling two little holes in the direction of their optic nerves. 'Optic nerve' contact means that you don't have to touch them and they are still experiencing your eye contact.

Avoid trying to force their face, with a firm torque on their jaw, to look towards you. This only results in a lot of yelling and upset and diverts everyone's attention from the request at hand.

Quiet, determined voice

By keeping your voice quiet, you are showing that you are in control of your voice and therefore in control of the rest of yourself. This 'control of you' ups the chances that you will be in control of your child and in control of the situation.

It is true that yelling at them may make them jump but you cannot be certain in which direction they are going to jump — towards or away from compliance.

Our children learn what they live and, if you yell at them, this generation of children will not hesitate to yell right back. Before you yell, consider what it is that you are teaching them. If it is not self-restraint and self-control, you probably don't want to be modelling it.

So say, quietly and powerfully, 'I want you to do [whatever it is] now, please!'

Compliance or non-compliance?

There are only two options at this point. Your child does as asked — or doesn't.

(There is a possible third category. Your child may do as asked very slowly or do half a task or do it very badly. I recommend that you don't think of this as a separate option. Just put it in the category of sabotage — an elegant but recognisable 'I'm not going to do as you say'.)

If you have taken all the trouble to stop what you were doing and/or get out of your chair and firmly and quietly TELL your child what is expected and they don't, they have decided 'No way'. To put it even more bluntly, they have decided 'Up yours'.

Although your child is not using these words — at least I hope not; and if they are we will deal with it in the chapter about household rules (see page 141) — they might as well be saying, 'Up your nose with a rubber hose. I have no intention of doing as you have asked'. Even more bluntly, their actions are saying 'Screw you'.

I apologise for the blunt and crude language. I just want you to realise that, if you have demonstrated the sort of power I am suggesting (space invade, height advantage, optic nerve contact and a quiet, determined voice) for a reasonable request and your child is still not complying, they are being incredibly rude to you.

Ways of saying 'No way'

I have declined to put into bold typeface Ways of saying 'Up yours' because I just couldn't go that far, but that is the intended title of this paragraph.

It is unlikely that your child will use the words 'No way' or 'Up yours', but their refusal to comply means just that. How is your child likely to show you that they have no intention of complying? It depends on their style of non-compliance. Where it is Sad, Mad or Distancing they are likely to use the same strategy as when saying 'No' — only much stronger.

Sad 'No way'

If your child uses sadness to show you that they have no intention of complying, they are likely to get very upset. They may increase the level of their whining, cry or collapse to the ground with grief. They may protest how unfair you are being and insist that they do everything in the household. Really artful ones may go so far as to say that you don't love them or that you hate them. They are having a very good go at sidetracking you.

No matter how pitiful their response, keep in mind how far out of proportion it is to a reasonable parental request to lie still while they are being changed, or to get dressed or clean their teeth or give you a hand with the dishes.

Every now and again, I get a phone call from a parent asking if a seven-year-old can be suicidal. I take this very seriously because clearly I would never want to ignore a child in agony. However, usually when I ask for the context of the comment, it is after a prolonged conflict over some tiny and reasonable request for compliance that has culminated with the child saying, 'I wish I were dead.' Is this child choosing death over drying dishes? I don't think so. The child has learned a very powerful way of getting the parent off-track from the original request.

Angry 'No way'

If your child uses anger as a means of avoiding compliance, he is likely to get extremely angry at your insistence that a task be done. He may shout at you, 'I told you I'm not going to do it' or 'You are so-o-o mean' or 'Why can't [whoever he nominates] do it?'

If you are a peace-loving parent it is hard to stay strong with a barrage like that. If you are an angry sort of person yourself, it is hard to stay the adult in a situation like that and not get sucked into a yelling match or use threats or force to get your child to comply. If you work hard at being a good parent, it is not easy to listen to your child yell, 'I hate you and I'm not going to be your friend'.

Our job as parents is to recognise that, despite the power and the anger that our child is showing, they are simply trying to get out of a small — in the scheme of things — parental request. It is hard to remind ourselves that it is good for our children to do as they are told so that they learn to tolerate the frustrations of life and start to develop the self-discipline required for mature young adulthood.

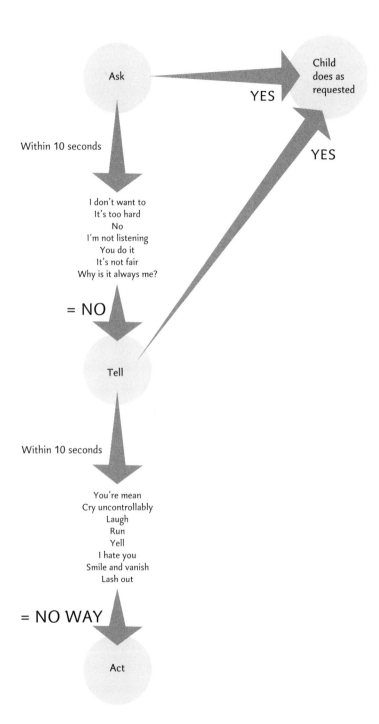

Distancing 'No way'

The child who 'distances' from our request may run off and hide, may look agreeable and say 'Yes, Mum' and appear to go off in the right direction, but they never complete the task. They may even look up at you with a charming grin and just laugh at you.

Particularly with the charming approach, it is quite hard to convince ourselves that not only is our child being non-compliant, they are being out-and-out (albeit in a charming way) rude and disrespectful.

We know within ten seconds

If we have ASKed once, then taken the trouble to stop what we are doing to go over and TELL our child what we expect, we will know within ten seconds of getting there what has been the outcome.

In response to a simple request there are only two answers. Yes — which our child would show us by doing as asked — and anything other than doing as told, which we can regard as a 'No way'.

ASK, TELL, NOW WHAT?

Once we have asked our child to do something, once we have moved into their space and insisted that they comply, there are only two possible outcomes. Either our child does as requested or they don't. If they do, an appropriate response would be 'Thank you for your help'.

If we have been through ASK and TELL and our child is not responding to our request, we need to do something about it. We need to ACT. We need to respond in a way that is powerful and effective. If possible, we also need to respond in a way that keeps the problem with our child and does not invite resentment or thoughts of revenge.

I have found that the most effective, powerful and appropriate response is a carefully planned and thought-through version of Time Out. So let's discuss Time Out.

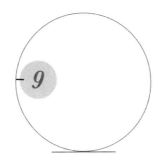

LET'S TALK
ABOUT TIME OUT

FROM TIME OUT AS PUNISHMENT TO . . .
SOMETHING ELSE

When I first started training to work with parents, I was taught to use basic behavioural psychology strategies. There were two extremes of a continuum. At one end was praise and positive attention. At the other end of the continuum was, Time Out as punishment.

Somewhere in the middle was 'planned ignoring', seen as the total absence of any positive reinforcement as a way of making undesirable behaviour go away. There were also natural and logical consequences, e.g. children fighting in front of TV are denied access to the TV for a number of days.

All of these methods were feasible and often ultimately worked. They did, however, involve enormous effort, dedication and consistency — often more than parents could muster up — and always felt, to me, as if I was imposing something on my children to make them do something.

Once I began to understand that Emotional Support was an effective way of connecting with and supporting our children's feelings, I began to wonder whether this was part of a different continuum and, if so, what was at the other end.

Then one day, I had a BFO (Blinding Flash of the Obvious): the opposite of Emotional Support is Emotional Distance!

TIME OUT AS EMOTIONAL DISTANCE

From time immemorial, people have used emotional distance to show that certain behaviours are displeasing. There is no more powerful force to use on human beings, who have a great need to 'belong' to a social group, than to exclude them from a social group they want to be with. It is not hard to remember back to schoolyard days and recall how hurtful and upsetting it was when someone said, 'You can't play with us.' We would do almost anything to get back in with the social group.

It began to dawn on me that Time Out is so effective not because children hate their rooms but because of their need for parental support and comfort and their need to feel part of the family. We didn't need to use the coal cellar with the spiders or the perfectly lit but unentertaining room or even the naughty chair. Being excluded from the family was powerful enough. The child then had the opportunity to decide to behave in ways appropriate for a family member.

TIME OUT FROM OUR SOCIAL GROUP

We've all been led to believe that children seek parental attention and that much inappropriate behaviour can be labelled 'attention seeking'. I have real trouble with this term because the implication is that the parent is not giving the child enough attention and, if only they would give the child more (positive) attention, the child's behaviour would improve.

This is far from my experience. In most families that I see, the children have more than enough attention and yet they continue to misbehave.

I believe that even more powerful than our need for attention is our need for parental support and the intrinsic feelings of 'rightness' when we behave according to the norms of our social group. Viewed this way, it is not surprising that our brief withdrawal of parental emotional support in Time Out is very meaningful.

Given that we largely parent on our own in separate houses (so our child's social group for the day may be as small as one parent), it is also not surprising that Effective Time Out is powerful because it means withdrawal from the available social group.

When children hit, bite, spit, swear or scratch and we use an Effective Time Out, we are giving them a clear message that this behaviour is not accepted in this social grouping. Similarly, when our children refuse to do as they are asked, or refuse to stop doing something they have been asked to desist from, they need to be excluded from the family team until they see it their parents' way.

TIME OUT FOR THE SMALL STUFF

Remember we are not asking our children to do something difficult or unreasonable. We are talking about ordinary, everyday requests of the order of:

- *Put on your socks.*
- *Leave the cat alone.*
- *Don't spit.*
- *Give me a hand with the dishes.*

Even though we may have a child yelling and screaming (much rarer when we use Time Out with an Effective Time Out attitude), it is important to keep in mind that, regardless of the volume or the upset, we are not tormenting our child but merely requesting simple, reasonable and age-appropriate tasks.

TIME OUT TO STRUGGLE WITH THEMSELVES

If we think about Effective Time Out as the absence of Emotional Support — in other words Emotional Distance — we have a way of leaving our children to struggle with their internal conflict of 'I don't want to do this; it looks as if I might have to.'

The beauty of this approach seems to be that, although children are not always happy about the idea that they have to comply with simple, reasonable parental requests, our children don't wind up resentful and vengeful because there is no anger, argument or punishment.

Children need space to struggle with themselves. Thus, the purpose of Effective Time Out is not to punish a child. It is to provide a quiet, safe space for children to wrestle with the issue of wanting to do things their way versus the need to be part of the family. This means it doesn't matter if a child says, 'I like it here.' It simply means she has not yet resolved the issue of whether to do as required and join the family or stay away from the family a bit longer.

This is her issue to resolve and, in the end, because of her social needs, the child will opt for the family. We have given her the space and respect to work it out for herself. When our child has decided she wishes to be part of the family and that taking two cups to the sink is a pretty fair trade for all the benefits that come with being a family member, she will emerge from her room and do as she is asked. Until she has reached this conclusion, we are wise to keep out of the way.

TIME OUT IS NOT A PUNISHMENT!

In order for Time Out to be effective, it needs to result in our child doing as told. Most important of all, we need to avoid our child feeling punished, mainly because punishment often leads to feelings of anger, dislike and revenge.

In order to avoid Time Out as punishment, we need it to happen in such a way that, instead of our child struggling with us, they only have themselves to battle with.

TIME OUT IS NOT A ROOM

Though in practice we may often wind up sending our children to their room, popping them in a corner or keeping out of their way, if we want Time Out to be effective, we need to give up on the idea of a naughty chair, a thinking spot or a punishment room or giving them 'the silent treatment'.

Effective Time Out is a state of mind. Time Out happens when we think, 'I have asked you to do something. Nothing much is happening between you and me until that is done.'

Parents of older children often tell me, 'I can't keep my child in her room' or 'It is too hard to send her to her room.' Clearly there comes a time when it is inappropriate and often impossible to confine our child to a particular spot. That is where thinking about Effective Time Out not as a room but as a state of mind becomes really useful. If we think of Time Out from our Emotional Support rather than Time Out in a particular place, then *we* can become the Time Out by keeping out of the way of our child. Time Out is over when *we* emotionally reconnect with our child.

THE GST APPROACH

Another powerful way of thinking about Time Out is the GST approach. Think to yourself (I recommend that you never give away your game plan to your child), 'There will be no Goods or Services from me to you until you have done as I have requested.'

For example, your teen has become cross about something you have done and has sworn at you. Far more powerful than growling, explaining, threatening or demanding an instant apology, we are much more effective when we say quietly and strongly, 'That is totally unacceptable. Let me know when you are ready to apologise', and then quietly go about our own business. We have handed the problem to our child and become 'Time Out'. Our child now has a problem to solve if she is ever going to have access to the goods and services that we normally provide. Let's leave her to solve the problem.

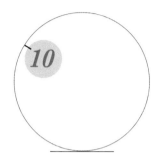

HOW POWERFUL DOES TIME OUT NEED TO BE?

We need to do something that shows our child we mean what we say and that nothing else is going to happen (in the way of goods, services, attention or support from us) until that is done.

We've talked about Emotional Support — supporting our children's feelings when they are upset, unhappy or angry. When they are feeling this way they are entitled to our support.

Likewise, when we make a simple parenting request, we are entitled to their compliance. Until they do as they are asked, a state of Emotional Distance, in other words Time Out, will exist until they have changed their mind and are ready to do as we have asked.

HOW MUCH POWER DO YOU NEED?

When you think of each child that you are responsible for, you will probably be able to think of how much power is needed to get them to change their minds. Our aim is to pitch it just right. Too powerful and you overwhelm your child — either with upset or with resentment. Not powerful enough and your child will have little or no respect for you or your actions.

Think of it as a continuum — from least powerful to most powerful. How much power do you need?

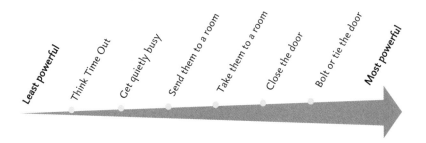

Think Time Out

The least powerful — but still tremendously effective Time Out — is when you change your thoughts about the situation.

I remember a time when I was busy at the kitchen sink and one of my (teen) children was standing at the end of it, chatting to me while I worked. The conversation clearly did not go the way she wanted and she was somewhat terse and rude. I remember going quite 'still' inside, thinking, 'You rotten little toad. That is no way to talk to a mother. I don't feel like ever talking to you again. In fact, I cannot think of a single thing I ever want to say to you or do for you.'

I stayed silent and as far as I can tell nothing in particular showed on the outside.

It probably took no more than a minute but it seemed like a very long time when, from her: 'Sorry, Mum. I was way out of line.' I assume she must have experienced the Emotional Distance (Time Out). Episode over without a word from me.

When I think about this, and the many other times that I have been so angry at something that one of my children has said or done that I knew that growling, yelling, explaining, demanding an apology or punishing was going to be much too much like hard — and probably ineffective — work, I am amazed at just how effective it is.

'Thinking Time Out' has the advantage that we keep the problem with our child, we don't suffer the indignity of losing our temper, and we respect our child's ability to know how to correct a situation.

The disadvantage could be that our child doesn't notice our change of attitude. In that case, we need to consider two possibilities:

1   For Think Time Out — or for any other form of Time Out for that matter — to be really effective, it has to happen in a climate of, and in contrast to, our unconditional emotional support of our child. So if we are grumpy and distant from our child most of the time, we shouldn't be surprised if our suddenly deciding to Think Time Out goes unnoticed. In this case, we need to be more attentive to our children's feelings and find more opportunities to support their feelings. That way, they may notice if we don't!

2   The second reason that Think Time Out may not work is if we have under-pitched the amount of power we need. We can either crank it up then or note that next time we are in the same situation, we will need to act more powerfully.

Get quietly busy

You tell your toddler that it is time to change his nappy or time to get into his high-chair. He runs away and parks his little backside in the nearest corner. You quietly go about doing whatever it is you need to do in the same room. You neither talk to him nor do you move towards him. You keep your shoulder slightly turned away so that all he sees is your back. Within a small amount of time, you can almost guarantee you will have a little person turning up next to you with arms outstretched going 'Up, up' and ready to do as you have asked.

Your school-age child or teen is always running late to leave the house for you to give him a lift to school or get to a sporting or cultural commitment. You've tried nagging, screaming, cajoling and threatening to leave him behind. Nothing helps.

Instead, try going about your business getting yourself ready and leaving him to it. At first he may not even notice, but there is something about that sort of purposeful silence emanating from a parent who is 'getting quietly busy' that seems to permeate through walls. Often, our child will simply show up to check that we are still in the house: 'If she's not nagging, she can't be there.' You're experiencing the power of 'getting quietly busy'.

If you feel that you must say something, avoid commenting on his lack of progress. There are two sorts of progress reports that you can give him instead:

1   Report on your progress. 'I am going to get dressed.' (This indicates about twenty minutes to leaving time.) Then, 'I am going to clean my teeth.' (This indicates about seven minutes to leaving time.) 'I am putting on lipstick.' (This one is usually for Mums only — about 30 seconds to leaving time.) 'I am ready to go.'

2   Report on the school's progress. 'We need to leave in twenty minutes if I am going to get

you to school on time.' 'We need to leave in
ten minutes if I am to get you to school on
time.' 'We need to leave in five minutes if I am
to get you to school on time.' 'We need to leave
now if I am to get you to school on time.'

At this point either you take your car keys and a newspaper and
sit quietly at the kitchen table, reading, or you go and sit in the car
without a word. Most children find the silence eerily disconcerting
and begin to take on their own responsibility of getting ready. You
may be able to get him there on time. You may not. Either way, he
will learn from the experience.

At every parenting seminar, when I suggest this, there is always
the question asked, 'But what if he is late for school?' The answer
is, 'What if he is late for school?' Hopefully he will be made to feel
sufficiently uncomfortable that he will choose not to experience that
situation the next time. What if he has a lovely, kind teacher who just
says, 'Oh, that's all right'? I would recommend a private word with
the teacher to tell her what you are trying to achieve. Ask her if, the
next time he is late, she could give him a bit of a 'rev-up'.

The next question is likely to be, 'But what if I have other
children to get to school?' Don't go near your delaying child, but
do reassure the others that you will keep them out of trouble and
take full responsibility for their lateness. When you eventually get to
school, start with the youngest and take them to their classroom. As
you greet the teacher, excuse them with, 'I am so sorry that they are
late. It was circumstances beyond their control.' Let the 'running the
family late' child take care of his own explanation.

ASK–TELL–Get quietly busy

With older children, when it is not suitable to send them or take
them to their room, it pays to keep in mind how much they need
our goods and services. Keeping quietly busy can be a very Effective
Time Out.

We've ASKed our child to do something; we've moved over and

TOLD our child to do something. Nothing much is happening. It is time to ACT and the action is Time Out — Time Out from all your goods and services.

A few months ago, I was to appear on a morning TV programme. Just before we went on air, the host said to me, 'I'd like you to come up with one quick tip for parents of teenagers.' What was the tip? 'Always remember that your teens need your support — and your goods and services — more than you can possibly imagine. And always remember, they cannot make *you* do anything.'

The important thing is, once you have ASKed and TOLD, you must be clear in your own mind that nothing else in the way of goods or services is going to happen until the task is done. Also, be determined that you are not going to hook into a vicious cycle of arguing, nagging, persuading, threatening or punishing.

You want your teen to give you a hand with the dishes. You ASK him and nothing much happens. You go over to him and TELL him. He says, 'Sure, Mum' and vanishes. It is time to ACT and that action needs to be an Effective Time Out. Get quietly busy on anything — except doing the dishes, of course. It may take ten minutes, it may take half an hour, but sooner or later your teen will need something from you.

'Mum? Do you know where my socks are?' 'Of course, sweetheart. First let's do the dishes and then I would be happy to find your socks.' Don't expect him to be delighted. Expect him to stomp off with some derogatory remark. This is a good time to pretend that you are deaf.

Guaranteed in another ten minutes he will be back with another request. 'Mum? Can you give me a lift to soccer?' 'Of course, darling. First let's do the dishes and then I would be delighted to drive you to soccer.' He is probably going to be very cross and stomp off once again or blame you for letting his team down, but soon it is going to dawn on him that you mean what you say and nothing much in his life is going to happen until he is ready to do as he is asked.

But what if you are in a hurry? There is more about this on page 176. For the moment, let's remember that this is not about some magic trick or punishment that is going to work three minutes before you leave the house. Getting our child to do as told requires enormous restraint and consistency on our part, and training and practice on our child's part.

The end point that we are after is that our children say 'Yes' automatically to simple requests and, of course, we would really appreciate the point beyond that when our children develop initiative to do what needs to be done for their own wellbeing. Beyond that, we are preparing children to have enough initiative to see what needs to be done and to be helpful volunteers, both within and outside the family.

SEND them to a room

When we use the 'Go to a room' concept, it is a metaphor rather than a particular place. In practice, it will often be that the child's room is the most suitable spot.

The go to your room metaphor is more powerful than Thinking Time Out or getting quietly busy. We are insisting that our child leaves our presence and goes off someplace else. We are increasing the Emotional Distance. We are expecting him to take himself off there and to stay there until he is ready to comply. It is a more powerful Time Out in that we are implying that we do not want him in our sight and we really don't want to hear from him either until he is ready.

To send a child away from where his parents are is a powerful way of showing him that he is expected to do as he is asked and that he is not welcome back until he is ready to do that.

TAKE them to a room

Now, let's start to consider what level of power we need for the child who is reluctant to go to a Time Out spot. If we have told them to go and they are not going, we need to do something about it. If we let it go at this point, we are just teaching them that they don't really need to do as they are told because they can rely on us to have no follow-through.

The simplest way with a toddler or little child is just to scoop them up and pop them in their cot or room. (Rather inelegantly, I tend to refer to this as 'scoop and dump'.) Say once, 'I'll be back to see if you are ready to do as Mummy has asked you', and leave.

With older or stronger children, leading them by the hand works. Basically, if you take their hand and head off in the right direction with swift confidence, the rest of their body is bound to follow. Some parents find it far more effective to 'lead from behind' and manoeuvre their child that way. Swift and sure is the most efficient way to go.

Avoid at all costs getting into a 'dragging and gripping of doorways' battle. If this is what happens when you take your child to Time Out, there are several things to think about:

1   Have I ASKed, moved into his space and TOLD him what to do in less than 30 seconds, or is this a long, drawn-out screaming match that has been going on for ten minutes or even half an hour? If it is the latter, you have lost so much power that your child is probably going to be impossible to get there. Resolve next time to ASK–TELL–ACT.

2   Have I been letting him get away with all sorts of things or been whining and bleating but not doing anything about it, then suddenly had enough and pounced? You are using Time Out as a punishment for getting to the 'last straw' rather than teaching your child that you expect him to do as he is told to simple requests . . . all the time.

3   Does my child have little respect for me in general and is he just treating this as 'Mum or Dad is trying something else out on me. What's the way around it?' Consider how often you get into the vicious cycle of yelling,

debating, threatening and arguing, and plan to
shift into a calm ASK–TELL–ACT response
to non-compliance.

4   Is dragging my child up or down a stairway
too difficult? Resolve to arrange Time Out
spots on each level.

With children too old to take — and you will notice that I have
squirmed away from nominating a particular age — you are better
off getting quietly busy and remembering the GST approach of no
goods or services until the task is done.

Why am I not prepared to commit to an age range? Parents
with little authority and no clear plan about how they are going to
raise their children to become self-disciplined adults may well have
trouble taking a four-year-old to their room. Parents with powerful
boundaries around their children's behaviour may well be able to say
to their eighteen-year-old, 'Buzz off. You're being impossible', and
the child will go off to a quieter spot and return ready to apologise
and be a civil human being.

In all cases, if we discover that we have gone about using a Time
Out room in a less than effective way, we always have the ability to
retreat to getting quietly busy and using ourselves as the Time Out
rather than the indignity of trying to haul them off to a place they
are not going to go to or stay in.

Close the door

If taking our child to his room and leaving him there to come
out when he is ready to behave is not powerful enough to get the
behaviour change we want, our Time Out becomes more powerful
and effective when we close the door.

This has the effect of showing our child that we do not want
him back in our lives until he is ready to behave. It also spares us
the agony of watching our child puddle around in his room, rolling
round on the floor, playing quietly or getting destructive — and it

makes sure that our child cannot torment us by making us watch him or listen to him.

It is a physical way of demonstrating that Time Out is occurring, we are not part of it and our child needs to struggle with 'I don't want to do it; it looks like I might have to' on his own until he has come to the right conclusion.

If your child does not respect a closed door, has no intention of complying and keeps coming out to annoy and irritate you, you may need to crank up Time Out to a higher lever of power.

Bolt or tie the door

If you take your child to his room and tell him to stay there until he is ready to comply, close the door and walk away . . . and your child keeps strolling out, he is being both defiant and cheeky. His behaviour is saying, 'Up your nose with a rubber hose. Up yours, I can do as I like. Screw you, I don't have to do anything you say.'

I do apologise for the rudeness of the language. I am wanting you to feel just how rude your child is being by strolling out of the room and letting his behaviour tell you that he has no intention of taking any notice, or if he has any intention of complying it will be at *his* wish, in *his* time, so there, take that.

If you find yourself in this situation with a child under ten (I can't imagine that this would do any good for your relationship with an older child), you will be amazed at the power of installing a high bolt or tying the door handle to the next door with a bungee cord.

Put the bolt up with great pomp and ceremony without describing its purpose. ('What's that for, Dad?' 'You'll see.') Don't threaten or explain. The next time you take your child to Time Out, say 'I'll be back to see you when you are ready to behave' or 'Call out when you are ready to do as I asked you to do' and wander off. Now your child really has a problem to solve.

What about holding the door?

You have put your child into his room. You have closed the door and are holding the handle, leaning out using your body weight so your child cannot force it open. Just who do you think is trapped?

Your child knows that you are there. You are standing, he may well be sitting down relaxing or all his frustration may be aimed at the door. The odds are that he finds your holding the door rather provocative.

Above all, if an Effective Time Out is supposed to be about Emotional Distance, we are not doing a good job if all our thoughts are beaming in through the wood panel, 'Just how long do I have to stand here holding the (expletive of your choice) door handle till Lord Muck in there makes up his mind?'

Give yourself a break, use the bolt, go away and make yourself a cup of coffee. Now that's what I call Time Out!

PLACES AND AGES
FOR TIME OUT

There are lots of differing opinions about the best place for an Effective Time Out. Some of these range around what place is the most powerful punishment. It won't surprise you, by now, that I am averse to thinking about Time Out as a form of punishment.

Other views conflict over which places in the house are supposed to be pleasant and which unpleasant. I am often asked if a child's room isn't supposed to be associated with pleasant rather than unpleasant feelings.

There is also the question of when is our child old enough for us to start to use Time Out, and when do they get too old. Let's address some of those issues.

FOUR STEPS TO TIME OUT AND COMPLIANCE

1   The first step is when we start thinking about our children's inappropriate behaviour and develop a plan — in this case, a plan to use Time Out for inappropriate behaviour.

2   The second step is when our brain registers that a particular unacceptable behaviour is occurring or has occurred and we need to action the plan.

3   The third step is when we carry out our plan and create a Time Out situation, by removing our positive regard and support, removing our child or removing ourselves.

4   The fourth and final step only occurs when our child has carried through and remedied the situation.

TIME OUT IS ALREADY HAPPENING WHEN WE CHANGE OUR MINDS

The first place that Time Out happens is in our minds. We see a particular behaviour that is inappropriate. We have already tried all sorts of positive ways (discussion, encouragement, praise, stickers) to change it, but to no avail.

We have resolved that the next time it occurs, we need to respond assertively to put a boundary around the inappropriate behaviour. We are going to respond to that behaviour by emotionally distancing ourselves from our child in some way.

The fact that we think, 'I am never going to tolerate that behaviour again without responding', or 'When I ask my child to do something, nothing else is going to happen until that is done', means the atmosphere in our house will already be changing.

TIME OUT IS ALREADY HAPPENING WHEN WE ARE CLEAR WHAT WE ARE GOING TO DO

After a counselling session or seminar discussing the particulars of Time Out, or hopefully after reading this book, parents go home very clear about exactly what steps they are going to take as soon as their child steps out of line.

Sometimes they don't get a chance to try Time Out for a few days. I suspect that when their child begins to behave inappropriately, the parent projects such a clear air of 'Don't even think about it' that the child has a change of heart. Don't worry. The opportunity will occur!

I tend to counsel in two-hour blocks and see clients at fortnightly intervals. Often the first appointment is spent gathering sufficient information to enable us to start talking strategies at the following one. I am frequently amazed and delighted when parents return saying, 'I don't know what happened, but our child's behaviour has greatly improved and we haven't done anything yet.' What has happened is that, as a result of spending time describing the behaviours and coming to terms with how bad they are for the child or for family life, the parents have gone home with a different mindset and that has been conveyed to the child without words.

HOW OLD DOES MY CHILD HAVE TO BE BEFORE I START?

Often this comes in the form of a question at seminars: 'Diane, when is my child old enough for discipline?' I translate that as: 'When is my child old enough to understand and respect boundaries?'

In order to answer this, we need to consider how our children develop a concept of what is acceptable or unacceptable behaviour.

Our babies can do nothing wrong. They feed, sleep or watchfully observe. They are driven by their innate needs and we do our best to meet those needs. They need our nurturing and our protection . . . and then they start to crawl! A whole new world of exploration opens up to them — a whole new world to crawl over and smell, taste, feel, lift, drop, throw and possibly destroy. Their behaviour is still not wilful, but there are some things we would rather they did not do.

I would love to think that we could teach them solely through positive means. When I was really keen on the power of positive attention, I thought it would be possible to raise a child without ever saying 'Don't', focusing solely on what I wanted her to do and ignoring the things that I didn't want her to do. Instead of 'Don't touch that' and 'Leave it alone', I would focus on when she stopped: 'Good girl for leaving it alone.'

Deb was at that wonderful stage when the parent jams all the books into the shelves so tight that adults can't get them out, but a determined crawler with a persistent little finger can wiggle and rip. She would crawl over and start to dismantle and I would say a sharp 'NO'. She would stop and I would say, 'Good girl for stopping' and move her away.

By fifteen months, we were at that lovely stage when all the kitchen cupboard handles had rubber bands hooked between them in order to slow down a marauding toddler. One day we heard her trying to open a 'rubber banded' cupboard. She was pulling it towards her saying 'N-o-o-o' and then letting it jump closed, saying 'Good girl.' As she repeated the open-and-shut sequence she kept repeating,

'N-o-o-o-o! Good girl! N-o-o-o-o! Good girl!' This did not mean that she wasn't getting into the cupboard. It just meant that we had a tiny window of opportunity to intervene.

The message of the story is that, from a very young age, our children are capable of understanding that there are some things they are not supposed to do. Deb understood that she shouldn't be getting into the cupboard, but she did not yet have the self-restraint to stop herself for long.

The look

So the best answer I can give you to 'When are they old enough?' is 'When you get "the look".'

Picture the scene: There is a pot plant. Our crawler or toddler wanders over to have a look at it. She looks at the front, she looks at the back, she sniffs the leaves, she tests the leaves for taste, bendiness and strength. She runs her fingers through the soil. She is focused on what she is doing.

This is the normal exploratory behaviour of a crawler or toddler. She can't tell what the back looks like from the front. Until she has tried, she does not have the experience to know about smell, taste and flexibility simply by looking. She needs to find out for herself through all her senses.

However, we do not particularly want her destroying the plant in her scientific journey to discover its properties. We pick her up and take her away to do something more acceptable. We repeat this several times over several days.

Now picture another scene: Our toddler advances upon the hapless pot plant. We have told her before, several times on several different occasions, that she is to leave it alone. As she reaches for the plant, she turns around to look at us with a cheeky smile and a challenging eye. The smile says, 'I know I am not supposed to be doing this. I am so-o-o cute. What are you going to do about it?'

We have just experienced 'the look'. She knows exactly what she is doing. This child (who may be any age from nine months to eighteen months) is old enough to be taught that when a parent asks her to do something or to stop doing something, that is what is happening next.

SWOOP AND SCOOP

The mildest type of Time Out, suitable for a crawler or toddler who has just given us 'the look' or who has repeatedly gone and touched things that we have repeatedly said 'No' to, is 'Swoop and Scoop'. We swoop over, pick her up and remove her to another bit of the room, saying firmly, 'Leave the pot plant alone', then engage her in some other activity.

We may need to do this a few times on one day or a few times over several days. If after that our child leaves the object alone, we can consider that Swoop and Scoop Time Out has been effective.

SCOOP AND DUMP (GENTLY)

Some of our crawlers and toddlers are more persistent. They think that Swoop and Scoop is a lovely game. In this case you may need to upgrade to 'Scoop and Dump'.

Our toddler or crawler keeps heading back to something she clearly knows she is not supposed to do (you've had 'the look' repeatedly). She has shown us that Swoop and Scoop is not powerful enough to teach her to give up on the behaviour.

We need a Time Out spot. A corner, a chair or a rug are all suitable, provided that our child stays there. Sometimes we may need to keep a restraining hand on her shoulders.

We pop her in the Time Out spot and say firmly, 'You know you are not supposed to [whatever it is she is not supposed to do]' and leave or hold her there until we are confident she has got the message.

This is the way I currently respond to my grandson (three) shoving his sister (two). It works well for me as a grandmother as I don't have to leave the room, my grandson is willing to stay put and it is powerful enough that he is unlikely to repeat the behaviour in under ten minutes. If I need to repeat it, it does not involve huge effort.

I recommend that you use this method first but, if it is not powerful enough — and you will know this after a couple of attempts — be prepared to upgrade to a spot where your child cannot get away.

I cannot begin to imagine that it would have worked with my own children. They would never have stayed put. It would have been a wriggly struggle to get them there and an even greater struggle to keep them there. I always found a cot much more effective.

THE COT AS TIME OUT

The cot is a splendid Time Out for children who can not yet easily 'leg it out'. Even if they can clamber out, it does give you a brief respite to get away or to close the door.

If our child is wriggling and turning while we are trying to change her or dress her, popping her in her cot with a terse, 'I'll be back to see if you are ready to hold still' is a powerful way of showing her you are not here to be teased, taunted or tangled with.

When our child repeatedly touches pot plants, hot stoves, forbidden electronic equipment, unwitting baby siblings, granny's glasses or the myriad other things that she needs to learn not to do, scooping her up and gently dumping her into her cot and walking out is an Effective Time Out.

Same place: different mother

You may be wondering if a cot is an appropriate Time Out — after all, isn't her cot supposed to be her happy, safe place where she sleeps? This is true. It is the same place where she sleeps. But I am a completely different mother when I put my child in a cot for sleep than when I use the cot for Time Out.

When I put my toddler to sleep in her cot, I am warm, soothing and full of emotional support. I am likely to be cooing, 'Come on, sweetheart, it's time for a lovely sleep. Let's say goodnight Daddy, goodnight teddy, goodnight mobile. Tuck you in, darling. Kiss for Mummy. Sleep tight.'

When my toddler is being deliberately obstructive or cheekily defiant, I scoop her up and pop her in her cot. My whole action is one of briefly distancing from her behaviour. Physically it is the same place, but emotionally it might as well be a different planet.

Final sales pitch for the cot — it is safe and it is easy on our backs.

GO TO A ROOM

Once the cot is no longer an appropriate place, a room or hallway is a good way of showing our child that we will not tolerate a particular behaviour. The features of an effective Time Out spot are much the same as a cot. It must be easy to use and close at hand, it must be safe and, if you're going to shut a child in, it needs to be escape-proof.

Some parents find me rather harsh when I talk about 'escape-proof'. If you put your child in a room and they stroll out or hop out the window unchecked, they are basically saying, 'Stuff you. I do what I like.' A small bolt on either door or window enhances your authority and your self-respect. If you are averse to either of these and provided your outdoor area is safe, keeping the doors shut so that our child has to seek permission to re-enter the house can also be an Effective Time Out.

But what if she likes her room?

As parents, it is pretty disconcerting when we open the door — expecting a contrite child desperate to join the family again — to be greeted with, 'Go 'way, Mummy. I like it here.' Equally potentially disempowering is the child who takes herself off to her room rather than complying. Just as you are about to declare powerfully, 'Go to your room', she says, 'I'm going to my room' and storms off, possibly slamming the door behind her. The third part of this 'she likes her room' concern is that our child often freely chooses to play in her room. How could that possibly be an Effective Time Out?

Punishment or Change your mind?

If you are thinking about Time Out as a deterrent or a punishment, any or all of the above scenarios would make your child's room an ineffective Time Out.

If, however, you are thinking about Time Out as a way of showing Emotional Distance, of demonstrating to your child that nothing else is going to happen until she is ready to comply or to behave appropriately, there is no problem if your child chooses to go to or to stay in her room. She simply is not yet ready and needs more time on her own to be ready to behave pro-socially and to join her family.

Trust the process. Sooner or later, she will need to be near you and she will be ready to 'trade' your Emotional Support for her compliance.

Is their room too entertaining?

Most of the time, a child's room is the simplest and best spot for Time Out. However, if you are not finding it powerful enough, consider just how entertaining their room might be. If it is loaded with distracting electronics, it is unlikely to be the best spot.

If our child is playing with available toys for a reasonable amount of time, she may well be settling her feelings sufficiently so that she can engage her thinking about how to behave. If she is submersing herself in the seductive, brain-absorbing world of electronics, I would consider the removal of TV, PlayStation, cellphone or iPod — or choosing a different place for Time Out.

If you are in the pre-teen phase, think very carefully before you load their room with electronics. If this is the room where they do homework, consider how many seductive distractions you are providing. Is this what you want to do, and can you think of a creative alternative? One possibility is to have TV, computers and electronic games in a public and communal space. This not only enables you to guard and protect your children from unsuitable information and entertainment, it also makes their choice of 'Stay in my room versus do as requested and get back to all the goods the family provides' so much faster to solve.

If our teens already have a room full of electronics to submerse themselves in, you will engender a huge amount of resentment if you suddenly have a 'clean out' or start confiscating the electronics. You are better off being pleasant and supportive when you get the opportunity so that when they retreat to their room and their electronics, there is something worth coming out for.

WHAT ABOUT 'NAUGHTY SPOTS' AND 'THINKING CHAIRS'?

If you are already finding these effective, stick with them. In fact, this is a good time to say to you, if you are doing something that is working for you and your family, don't let any so-called expert talk you out of it. If, however, you are struggling with compliance issues and the 'naughty spot' or 'thinking chair' isn't working for you, it may be time to look at another strategy or point of view.

I find that sending children to a room is more powerful, more effective and preserves our child's dignity better than a naughty spot or thinking chair. For a start, I am not keen on the words 'naughty' or 'thinking'.

Naughty spot or naughty chair implies that the child is naughty and that the child is being punished for 'naughty' behaviour. There are many behaviours that are mischievous, destructive, aggressive or sneaky that I would have no trouble labelling naughty. There are many children who deliberately do these things and I would not be averse to using the term naughty to describe them. However, what we are discussing is compliance and an attitude that says 'it may be OK not to want to do something, but nothing much else is going to happen until it is done'.

Thinking chair seems to imply that the child will go to the chair and think about her misdeeds and how naughty or unreasonable she has been. I don't think children do that. They may think about how to get away. They may sit there and yell or cry. They may sit there and plot revenge. They may spend their time falling off the chair so you have to come and put them back on. But if we imagine that they sit there thinking, 'I've been very unappreciative and unreasonable and my lovely parents don't deserve this and from now on I am going to be grateful and always do as they ask', I think we are being unrealistically optimistic.

BE PREPARED TO BE FLEXIBLE

It pays to be flexible if you have a determined child.

One of my younger daughter's lovely Time Out tricks as a four-year-old was to wet the carpet absolutely deliberately and then greet me with, 'Now look what you've made me do.' It took me a while to work out that the simplest solution was to shift the locus of Time Out to a place without carpet! That worked.

Years later, Deb told me that, if she needed to go to the toilet, she would very quietly whisper, 'I need to go to the toilet', so that when I surveyed the wet carpet and stormed, 'Why didn't you call me?' she could say, 'I called you but you wouldn't come.' Parenting in the real world is a huge advantage for a Family Therapist!

And when Deb was about five she had been having a wonderful time with papers, scissors and glue. It was dinner time and I needed fairly rapid access to the table. 'Deb, darling, could you please put all the scraps in the bin so that I can set the table?' 'Oh, Mum. I am too tired.' I knew full well that she was tired and that if I sent her to her room she would happily lie on her bed and play quietly and possibly fall asleep. 'Come with me, sweetheart,' I said, looking disarmingly harmless. I gently led her to a little changing area that we have in front of a shower-box. 'You just sit there until you are ready.' It took about five minutes until Deb, ever ready to save face, appeared and said cheerfully, 'Mum, you have no idea how refreshing that shower-box is. I'm ready to clean up now.'

TIME OUT IS A STATE OF MIND

Time Out is not a room or a cot or a coal cellar with spiders. Time Out is an attitude, a state of mind.

You know your child best. Choose the Time Out spot and the minimum amount of power most likely to work. If you have a sensitive, easily upset child who just needs a place to cry while she decides that she has no option other than to do as you have asked, sending her to her room is likely to be more than enough. If you have a strong-willed, repeatedly defiant child, the odds are that you are going to have to use a locked door.

THINK SAFETY AND PROXIMITY

When you think about what you are going to use as a Time Out spot, consider what is safe or what you have to do to make that spot safe. Also, think about proximity. For the child who storms off to her room, slams the door behind her, stays furious for a while and then returns cheerful and willing, it doesn't matter much how far away her room is.

For the child who will be difficult to get to a Time Out spot, you would be ill-advised to try to drag her up two flights of stairs and along a corridor. If our designated Time Out spot is too difficult to get to, we will find ourselves resorting to nagging, persuading and yelling — anything rather than facing the wriggling child and the flight of stairs.

In two-storey houses it is both sensible and useful to have a Time Out spot on each level.

TIME OUT FOR OLDER CHILDREN AND TEENS

You will notice that I am being very vague about when children are too old to send to their rooms. I am going to stay vague. However, there does come a time when it isn't appropriate. Way before that stage is reached, parents often say to me, 'I can handle them now — just — but I am worried about what I am going to do when they are older.'

As our children get older we still need to ask them to do things or to stop doing things. Luckily, they are still going to need our advice, our support, our goods and our services — so the same principle applies. When we ask our child to do something, we still anticipate that the next thing that will happen between our child and ourself is whatever it is we have asked for.

It is hard to control what our younger children do. It is virtually impossible to control what our older children do, nor is struggling with them a clever or appropriate idea.

We cannot make a fifteen-year-old move two cups to the sink. But we can decide that we are not going to get involved in her life until the cups are in the sink. It is not necessarily wise to announce it or threaten it. That way we are setting up a challenge. The simplest way, having ASKED and TOLD, is to get busy with our own things. Sooner or later our child will need something from us. We can say calmly, sweetly and without sarcasm or threat, 'First put the cups in the sink and then I'd be happy to help.' It may work. It may not. If not, Time Out in our mind still holds. Go about whatever you need to do, quietly powerful in the knowledge that you have asked for something to be done and you are not available until that is done.

Don't expect your child to be thrilled and cheerful. She may have found whining, nagging and tantrums worked in the past. She may be stunned or angered to discover that it isn't working any more. It may take her a while to get used to your calm, uninvolved approach.

Relax and remember that you have asked for a perfectly reasonable and simple task, well within your child's capability, to be done. Time Out — meaning cutting off your Emotional Support — holds until that simple task is done.

The only thing we have any real control over is our own actions. Let's leave the problem with our child and let her get on with reaching the conclusion that she needs to do as we have asked.

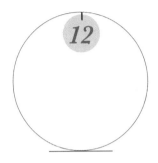

HOW LONG IN TIME OUT UNTIL THEY ARE READY?

It's time to revisit ASK and TELL and ACT.

- *We ASK our child to do something.*
- *We move over and TELL our child to do it.*
- *Our child declines the opportunity, so we ACT.*

The action is Time Out. We are going to get distance from our child or 'distance' our child from us.

This is a good time to remind ourselves what we are after. We have asked our child to do something or to stop doing something. He can comply right away. He can comply after we have moved into his space and told him what we expect. He can change his mind on the way there. He can change his mind after one second in Time Out. He can change his mind after one year there. (A slight exaggeration!) All we are requiring of him is that he change his mind.

Nothing much is going to happen until that is done. And when our child complies, we can stop biting our tongue and free it up to say 'Thank you.'

HOW LONG DOES TIME OUT LAST FOR?

Let's remind ourselves of why we are using Time Out. We no longer wish to get involved in a vicious cycle of nagging, persuading, debating, threatening and punishing. We want to set the situation up in such a way that our children have only themselves to struggle with.

From my point of view, once the Time Out has started, there are only two possible ways it can go. If our child is NOT READY to do as he is told, he needs to struggle a bit longer. Time Out holds. If our child is READY to do as he is told, he has resolved the struggle. Time Out is over.

'IF YOU, THEN I'
VERSUS
'WHEN YOU, THEN YOU'

One of the best ways of distinguishing between Time Out as punishment and Time Out as a place to change your mind was told to me during a seminar. (Thank you, Glenda.) It is the difference between 'If you . . . then I . . .' and 'When you . . . then you . . .'

When we use the threat of Time Out as a punishment ('If you . . . then I . . .') — for example, 'If you push your sister again, then I will put you in Time Out' — we have actually given our child a choice. They can continue with the behaviour and then go to Time Out or they can stop the behaviour.

Similarly, if we say to our child, 'If you don't do that (for example, put your shoes away), then I will put you in Time Out', many children would far prefer to be in Time Out than put their shoes away. Again, we have inadvertently offered up a choice that we may not wish our child to have.

Notice that, in each example, our child may prefer the punishment to doing as requested or stopping an undesirable behaviour.

Instead, let's use 'When you . . . then you . . .'

- *When you are ready to stop hurting your sister, then you are welcome to join the family.*
- *When you are ready to put your shoes away, then you are welcome to come out of your room.*

Notice that there is no punishment involved. There is a choice, but it is solely the choice of *how long* it will take our child to be ready to behave appropriately.

WHAT HAPPENS IF HE CHANGES HIS MIND ON THE WAY THERE?

Resist all desire to snarl, 'Too late. You should have thought of that sooner. You still have to go.' That would be punishing him for thinking about not complying.

He has done something much better than that. He has considered not doing as he is told and he has changed his mind. That is exactly what we have been trying to achieve. We want to hand the problem over to our child and give him the opportunity to solve it himself. He did — and very quickly too. It worked.

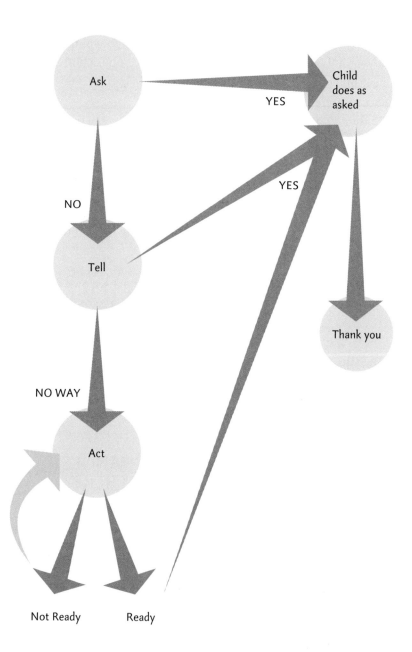

THE TEN-SECOND TIME OUT

If we are very lucky, we can use just a ten-second Time Out with a young child to make a point.

Our eight-month-old needs a nappy change. (In fact, our child will need hundreds of nappy changes till we get to the last one, so we might as well sort it out now.) We are getting sick of him leaving his head in the same spot but turning his body 180 degrees and then crawling off the end of the changing table. We are determined that we are never going to struggle with nappy changes again. I recommend starting with the first change in the morning and then never tolerating squirming again.

It is no use waiting till halfway through a poo-change and then using Time Out. If we know that a nappy change is likely to be difficult, we can just lie him down and wait for the beginning of the squirm. Scoop him up and say firmly, as you pop him in his cot, 'You know you are supposed to lie still while Mummy changes you.'

Walk away, out of sight and count slowly to about ten or until you hear him drawing breath, preparing to shriek. Just before he cries, pop in with a friendly voice and, put your arms out to him, saying, 'Are you ready to hold still for Mummy while she changes you?'

If he comes into your arms 'softly', i.e. co-operatively, he is Ready. Time Out is over. Change him, chat to him, give him things to hold, sing songs and enjoy his company. If he resists coming to you or changes his mind about lying still, he is Not Ready. Back to his cot. Walk out again, saying, 'I'll be back to see if you are ready to hold still while Mummy changes you.' Soon, he will be ready to be changed.

The important thing is not to begin taking off his nappy till he shows you he is willing to lie still during the entire change.

The term 'ten seconds' does not indicate a chronological time — although often as little as ten seconds is all you need to make your point — but a short amount of time, long enough to show your little one you mean business and nothing is going to happen until he is prepared to lie still and have his nappy changed.

SCOOP AND DUMP

Slightly stronger is the 'scoop and dump' approach. You ask your two-year-old to hold still while you put his shoes on. He doesn't want his shoes on. (This is not a situation where you can afford to have him learn by experience — it is freezing cold and there is broken glass!) As you approach him he begins kicking and flailing. You risk losing teeth.

Scoop him up and pop him in his cot or whatever Time Out spot you use. Say, 'I'll be back to see if you are ready to have your shoes put on' and walk out the door. He doesn't have to get seriously upset. Walk out and wait about fifteen seconds. Go back and ask, 'Are you ready now?' More often than not you will have made your point and your child will accept a cuddle on the way down to the ground and then be ready to co-operate. If not, go away for a bit longer, knowing that he is safe and in a position to come to terms with the fact that nothing else is happening in his life until he is willing to do as you have asked.

SCOOP AND WAIT

As soon as your child is old enough to walk out and comply or call out that they are Ready, all you need to do is scoop them off to Time Out. If your Time Out situation is one that your child can leave by himself, as you leave him say, 'As soon as you're ready to [do whatever it is that you've requested], you are welcome to join the family.'

If your Time Out situation is one that your child cannot leave by himself, as you leave him say, 'As soon as you're ready to [do whatever it is that you've requested], call me to say you're ready.'

How is your child likely to respond? Of course, ideally, he will think it over for a few seconds, indicate that he is Ready and it will all be over. You will have a co-operative child. Yeah right!

Let's not be too sarcastic. After a few experiences of Time Out until he is Ready, he will understand that once you have moved into his space and told him what to do, it's all over. Nothing much will be happening until that is done. He doesn't have a choice . . . well, that's not exactly true: he does have a choice. He can do as he is requested right away or he can do as he is told after ten seconds in his room (or ten minutes or ten years). What he will learn is that nothing much is going to happen until he is ready to do as requested.

TIME OUT STYLE

Whatever your child's way of saying 'No' — Sad, Mad or Distancing (see page 79) — you can expect their style of behaviour in Time Out to match.

Our child who gets sad when asked to meet simple requests, who moans and grizzles and wails 'I ca-a-a-a-n't', will raise his sadness level in Time Out. He will cry more loudly and more heart-wrenchingly. This is hard to listen to and you may need to go to the other end of the house. Keep remembering that you have not asked him to climb Mt Everest before breakfast; you have asked him to do some simple manageable task like clearing away some toys or packing his school bag.

Our child who gets angry when asked to do a simple task will get even angrier in Time Out. He may scream out, 'I hate you. You are the meanest Daddy in the whole world. It's not fair.' You may well hear the stamping of feet and the throwing of objects. He needs to get rid of a fair bit of rage in order to start thinking about what is necessary to do next.

Remember the Think–Act–Feel triangle (page 35) and try to imagine that he has to settle his feelings before he can get into a reasonable frame of mind. I know that we would all like to help our children to settle their feelings but, since we have 'caused' the feelings to get out of control by making a reasonable parenting request, we are disqualified from helping them settle their feelings.

Our child who uses distancing and delaying tactics rather than complying, will continue to do just that in Time Out. He will find toys to play with and, even if you put him in a toy-free area, he will find a piece of fluff or a leaf to occupy himself. Our hardest job is to accept that these children give you very little feedback that any change of mind is ever likely to occur. They will turn Time Out into an endurance test for you.

My best advice is for you to get busy and leave them to it. They need more time on their own than other styles of children and, for a start, will probably enjoy the peace. Eventually, their need to be with the people who provide them with Emotional Support will take over and they will be ready to comply.

All this begs the question, 'What if I am in a hurry?' I will address these and more in Chapter 16: 'Frequently Asked Questions about Time Out.'

WHEN TO INTERVENE

Whenever you hear any sound (or absence of sound!) that gives you any concern about your child's safety, never hesitate to intervene right away. It doesn't matter how good the strategy is, nothing is more important than your child's safety and wellbeing.

Most of the time when you go in, you will find your child safe, but in a still Not Ready state. Make some neutral comment, like 'Just checking to see if you are ready' and back out. Expect outrage.

Another time is when you hear that your child has gone into a dreadfully upset mode. Either they have gone from sad to very, very sad to 'so sad I cannot settle my feelings by myself' or, if they started in a mad or distancing mode, they have now switched to being dreadfully upset and need your support. The odds are they need your Boring Cuddle to settle their feelings. Don't hesitate to go into the room and offer a soothing, wordless cuddle. Once your child's feelings are settled, the odds are very high that they will be ready to do as asked.

SEND AND WAIT

Once your child is old enough to be sent off to his room or to storm off to his room, it really is a matter of waiting it out. It is not only about controlling your child's behaviour. It is also about respecting that many children need lots of down-time in a busy day.

If your child is spending extra long amounts of time getting ready to comply, there are a few things to consider.

1   Is the Time Out spot too pleasant and entertaining? If so, change the venue or remove some of the absorbing toys. If one of the absorbing toys is a cellphone, consider popping in with folded laundry to put away and hang around silently just being enough of a nuisance with your presence that your child can no longer continue the call.

2   Is my child exhausted or overwrought and Time Out is the best thing to happen in his day? Either accept that your child needs 'down-time' and leave him to enjoy it, or think about how much you are fitting into his day and consider some lifestyle changes or rearranging of priorities. (A question I often ask parents is: 'How many times a day is your child having to get in and out of a car?')

3   Have they become adolescent without our

noticing it and they like mooching in their room? The days of rapid compliance because they hate being away from you are over! Make sure that you make any time spent together as supportive or as pleasant as possible, so that at least your child notices your absence in his life rather than feels relieved.

Also, if you have not done so before now, begin to develop a good memory. You will need it for the child who emerges from his room, finished with Time Out but not necessarily ready to comply.

Looks like a Ready . . . but!

We have asked our child to take his plate and cutlery and put them in the sink. He has declined the opportunity. We have sent him to his room until he is ready. He has been there for a while. He calls out that he is ready and we open the door or he saunters out of his room. He comes into the kitchen or dining room, walks past the table and draws our attention to a drawing that is stuck to the fridge with a magnet. 'Who put that there, Dad?' he asks disarmingly.

Time for your memory to kick in. You asked him to do something, you told him to do something, he came out of his room, he looked ready to comply . . . but it has just turned into a Not Ready. Bearing in mind we are keeping the problem with our child, the smartest thing we can do is to state the problem that is his to solve. 'You've been asked to clear your plate and cutlery. You're obviously not ready. Off you go.'

He may go gracefully. He may resist or go muttering all the way. He may even change his mind at that point and decide that it is easier to do as requested now rather than add another round of Time Out in his room. That's fine. He's Ready to comply.

Our job is to remember that once we have ASKED him to do something and TOLD him to do something, nothing else is happening until he is Ready and has complied.

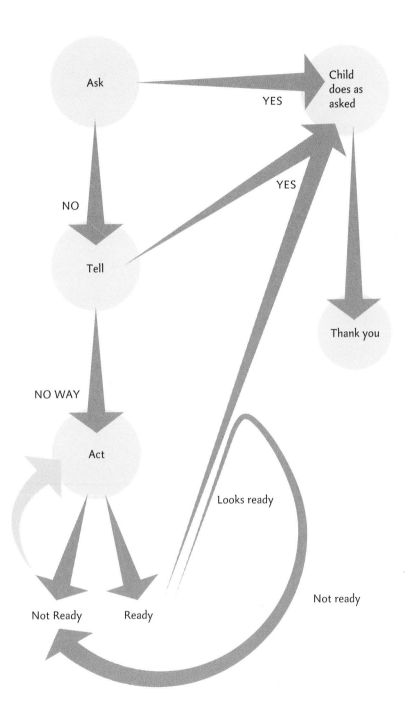

The various disguises of Not Ready

There are various responses to the anticipated offer of Time Out or to the offer of release from Time Out that parents find disconcerting.

Probably the most disconcerting is when we approach our child to tell him to do something or we have already invaded his space and told him what we expect and he announces 'I'm going to my room' or 'I'm going to Time Out' — and off he goes. Does it count as Time Out if our child chooses to go there? As I have said before, the answer depends on your attitude to Time Out.

If you are using Time Out as a punishment, you will experience it as not working if your child chooses to go there. If you subscribe to my view of Effective Time Out — an opportunity for a child to change his mind — then your child taking himself off to Time Out is just fine. He doesn't want to do as you have asked so he needs to be in Time Out until he changes his mind. He's just saved you the problem of getting him there.

Similarly, if our child rushes off to another place in the house or garden, he has just 'Time Out-ed' himself. Where he has gone is irrelevant unless it is loaded with electronic toys. Even then, eventually he will need your support and will return. Just stay alert to make sure that he does as asked upon his return.

Another child strategy that disconcerts parents is when we say 'Are you ready?' or 'You can come out now' and our child says 'No thanks, I like it here' or 'No thanks, I'm busy'. Stay cool. This is just another version of a child not being ready to comply. Wander off and leave them to it. Similarly with a child playing happily in their room. They are not yet Ready.

A third possibility is when you open the door to let your child out, expecting remorse and compliance, only to be met with 'Go away. You're a mean poo.' Stay cool. Say, 'Oh! You're not ready. Call out when you are', and leave him to it.

A fourth possible Not Ready response is when your child is distraught: 'I ne-e-ed a hug.' Give your child a silent cuddle and wait. In a short amount of time you will know if your child needed a cuddle to settle his feelings so he could get into a compliant frame of mind.

IF TIME OUT IS NOT A ROOM, HOW LONG DOES IT LAST?

When our children are too old or too powerful to send to their room, how do you tell when Time Out is over? It is exactly the same as if they were in a physical Time Out. Time Out is over when our children comply. We create a Time Out atmosphere by not being involved with our children until they have complied.

We are relying on the fact that our children need our Emotional Support or they need some of the goods or services that we normally provide.

We ASK and TELL our child what we want. They let us know that they have no intention of complying, either by refusing, complaining or wandering off in another direction. It is up to us to remember that we are the Time Out. Nothing much is happening until they comply. We go about our business. Not surprisingly, we often feel rather aggrieved that we are in this position again.

Our child stays away for a while and then comes into our orbit with some request. It is time for our long-term memory (that he is in Time Out) to kick in. We are better off acknowledging him, using good manners but not hooking into, re-explaining or problem solving. 'I'd love to do that for you as soon as you have done as you have been asked' invites a new argument around 'I can't remember . . .' 'Of course you can remember.' Our child mutters something as he stalks off — it pays to feign deafness here — or he may round on us with such nonsense as, 'Why won't you ever do anything for me?' Remember this is a 'try-on', not an impartial, expert assessment of your parenting commitment.

Our child returns with a different strategy: 'Dad, I have to be at soccer in ten minutes.' Bearing in mind that we have asked our child to put his plate and cutlery in the sink — or some other task that takes a short amount of time and a small amount of effort — keep the Time Out his problem. 'As soon as you have done as asked, I'll be ready to take you.'

YOU CAN'T MAKE THEM
DO ANYTHING . . . AND VICE VERSA

When our children are young, we have the power to physically make them do things.

We can pin a child down while we change them, we can bend them into their car-seat and snap the straps shut, we can keep putting them back to bed till they give up.

If we really want them to pick up a pile of blocks, we can make their hand wrap around each block and place it in their block box. (Disclaimer — not a strategy I would recommend.)

For every parent who is reading this and says, 'Diane, you are wrong. I can't make my child eat, sleep or go to the potty', I agree. These are areas that we cannot control through compliance strategies, nor should we. These are mainly aspects of physical development and maturation. And I will make some comment in a later chapter about how these intersect with compliance.

But for most compliance issues, we can make small children do as they are told.

With older children, we cannot make them do anything without their co-operation. However, it is important to remember that they cannot make us do anything we don't wish to do either.

They cannot make us drive them places, they cannot make us give them money, they cannot make us buy them alcohol, they cannot force us to give them driving lessons and they cannot force us to write false letters releasing them from assignments. (This list is by no means exhaustive!)

What about letting the team down?

One of our children's favourite forms of blackmail — when they had deliberately left compliance to a simple request 'too late' — was to bleat, 'But you'll be letting the car-pool and all of my team down!' That's an interesting concept. At that point, we had been driving our children to various team practices for ten years. We had stood on the sideline in freezing conditions for hours on end while they did handstands in between the goalposts, we mopped tears when they lost and bought celebratory milkshakes for the entire carload when one of them scored a goal. We paid endless fees, supplied countless oranges, spent a great deal of our supposed leisure time in A and E and they have the cheek to say — when they could have made their bed in under twenty seconds instead of battling us for two hours — *we* let the team down!

The speech I have just given is only useful in our own heads to remind us not to retreat or to justify. This is a good time to behave like a duck: calm on top and paddling like hell underneath. Repeat quietly, 'I'm ready to leave. The car will start as soon as your bed is made', sit down with a cup of coffee and a newspaper and you will be amazed how fast your child will be ready.

Provided you let the lesson speak for itself and not hook into blaming, explaining, threatening or excusing, your child will learn a valuable lesson without your having to say a word. It will be a very quiet ride to the practice.

EXTENDED TIME OUT
FOR OLDER CHILDREN

(otherwise known as 'You may not be able to stop them, but you don't have to give permission')

Often, we need to remind ourselves of the purpose of Time Out. Short term, it is a way of letting children learn that when we ask them to do something, our expectation that it will be done holds until *after* it is done. Long term, we are training our children to make wise decisions and this usually needs to happen through experience.

Often we have to endure quite a gap between our children being determined that they can do whatever they like and their discovering that it is not the most comfortable position in the world. At times like this, it may be of some small comfort to go back to the diagram on page 43 to convince ourselves again that we are keeping the problem with our child, so that they stay responsible for the solution.

The two stories that I am about to tell you both concern extremely good-natured children who were determined to do exactly as they pleased. They were both also very good negotiators and their parents had many experiences where the children persuaded them that this time would be different. That their parents mostly believed them was not so much bad judgement as 'the triumph of hope over experience'.

Example 1

Once upon a time there was a very gregarious fifteen-year-old. He just loved being with his friends. He would come home after school and immediately want to go out to be with his friends again. Since his mother expected him to do his homework, he had to be pretty creative. He would think of something he urgently needed from the local shops or some information from classmates that was essential to his homework and fervently promise to be back within twenty minutes. Often he would return three or four hours later.

As I talked with his mother, it became clear that he always managed to wangle her permission. ('Just this time. Just ten minutes.') There was no way his mother could or should have physically stopped him from leaving the house. However, it was important that she kept the problem with him rather than struggling over it with him. By refusing to struggle, she was making it entirely his problem.

The next time he started to come up with reasons why it was absolutely imperative that he leave the house after school, she simply said, 'Not with my permission.' Of course, once wasn't enough and he tried several ways of hooking her into his dilemma. She just stuck to 'Not with my permission.' When he pointed out that she couldn't stop him, she agreed that was so but she was not prepared to give permission.

He went and returned after an hour and a half. She acknowledged his return but stayed somewhat remote and cool for the rest of the afternoon and evening. Over the next few weeks, he sometimes went for a short time and more often didn't even bother asking or going. The combination of refusal to engage in fruitless discussion (emotional distance/Time Out), no permission (keeping the problem with the child) and polite coolness (emotional distance/Time Out) upon his return meant that he eventually gave up on his after-school escapades.

Example 2

Our own daughter went through a patch where, with my permission, she would meet up with a friend after school on the understanding that she caught a 5pm bus home. Somehow there was always something wrong with the bus (it was late, it was early, it broke down, it didn't ever arrive, it went the wrong way) and the result was I would have to go in busy traffic to pick her up.

How could I go about keeping the problem with her and use Time Out as emotional distance? I knew the theory, but how to apply it here? I knew that I had done all the arguing, debating, cajoling and threatening that I recommended others didn't! What was the alternative?

I sat her down and said, 'Deb, this has been going on for long enough. Every time there is a different excuse about the bus. I can't trust you to be on the bus you say you'll be on. There will be no more meetings after school until you show me that I can trust you to show up when you say you will.' I thought that this was a fine way of keeping the problem with Deb, but she had one more strategy left in her arsenal. 'But Mum! How can I show you that you can trust me if you won't let me go and come home by bus?'

'I don't know,' was my reply, mainly because I didn't! With hindsight, I now know that I was resisting getting hooked into problem solving and keeping the problem with Deborah. For three weeks there was a mildly hostile atmosphere whenever the topic came up. I refused to give permission; she couldn't think of any other way. (By the way, on all other matters I did my level best to be as pleasant as I possibly could be.)

After three weeks Deb came to me. 'Mum, you were right. I was missing the bus deliberately. If I catch the 4.30 bus which means that I should walk in the door at 4.55pm, would you give me a chance to show that you can trust me?' Notice that she took full responsibility for the situation and she came up with a resolution to the problem. It may not look like a conventional Time Out, but it was definitely Time Out from my support and services (solely on the subject of meeting her friend after school) until she was ready to take full responsibility.

TO SUMMARISE

Regardless of age, stage or personality style, our aim is to teach our children to do as they are told and that we mean what we say. For any request, we need to ASK once, move over to their space and TELL them what we expect, and then have the wisdom, patience and determination to recognise when our child is Not Ready and hold out until they are Ready (to overcome their frustration and take age-appropriate responsibility).

This is one of the more difficult tasks of parenting but one that sets up our children to grow into self-disciplined adults. Along the way, we will discover how pleasant it is to have a child who is relatively compliant, a person whose company we can enjoy and who is a pleasure to be with.

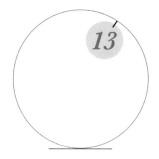

HOUSEHOLD RULES

Let's return to ASK–TELL–Time Out–ready to do as told. This is a great sequence for gaining compliance or getting our children to stop doing something that we disapprove of.

However, there comes a time when we hear ourselves beginning sentences with, 'If I've told you once I've told you a hundred times' and finishing with, 'Why can't you just stop doing . . .' This is a good indication that we are dealing not with non-compliance but with simple rule-breaking. Our children are doing things that they know they are not supposed to do.

ESTABLISHING HOUSEHOLD RULES

Parents often ask me if they should sit down with their children and agree upon rules and/or write down a list of rules to be placed in some prominent position. While either or both of these may be useful to show our children that we have committed to change, I am not sure that they are necessary. Be assured that your children know what the household rules are, they just don't obey them.

Imagine if I could interview your three-year-old:

> **Diane**: Are you allowed to hit your little brother?
>
> **Three-year-old** (*hesitating — pretty certain this is leading in an unpleasant direction*): N-n-n-o!
>
> **Diane**: Do you do that sometimes?
>
> **Three-year-old** (*still suitably cautious*): Y-y-es.
>
> **Diane** (*mischievously, with a twinkle in her eye*): Is it fun?
>
> **Three-year-old** (*with a big smile*): Yes!

So we have established that our three-year-old knows that she is doing something which she is definitely not allowed to do. All we have to do, to stop our three-year-old hitting her brother, is to respond appropriately and powerfully each time the behaviour happens.

Rules of the household

If we could interview our fourteen-month-old in the same way I described about wriggling and squirming while her nappy is being changed or pulling at electrical cords, I suspect that we would get much the same answer. And I also imagine that if we could interview our fifteen-year-old and ask whether she was allowed to use certain Anglo-Saxon words in the hearing of her parents, we would get much the same sequence.

So what sorts of things come under the heading of rules? Anything that you know is absolutely inappropriate. It is not appropriate for children to hit their siblings (or anyone else for that matter), to swear, to throw things, to play unkindly with the pets, to annoy a baby playing happily on the floor, to be verbally nasty, to tease people who cannot handle being teased, to snatch things out of the toddler's hands . . . and so on. These are behaviours that have no positive purpose and simply need to be stopped.

Rules are broken by any action or behaviour that our child absolutely knows that they are not supposed to do, but still persists in doing. How can we stop them?

RULE BROKEN — TIME OUT

Since we have told our children many times that this particular behaviour is unacceptable, we can skip ASKing them not to do it and skip TELLing them not to do it. We just need to respond immediately, each and every time.

Baby Time Out

When our babies are old enough to pull our ears, pull our earrings (it is easiest to take them off until our child is in kindergarten), climb our ribs or 'spare tyres' (depending on our body build), pinch or hit, it is a good idea not to dismiss it as compulsory baby behaviour. Instead, it is a good time to show our babies and toddlers that there are boundaries, that we will not allow our little one to treat us badly or to cause us pain.

The simplest Time Out for a sitter or crawler is to say strongly, for example, 'No hitting', while turning them around to face away or popping them on the floor. If they are indifferent and amble off to do something else, at least we have made our point. If they are upset, allow a ten-second pause to make your point. Then pick them up and comfort them.

If they immediately repeat the behaviour, pop them down a second time — just to show it is not some random behaviour on your part.

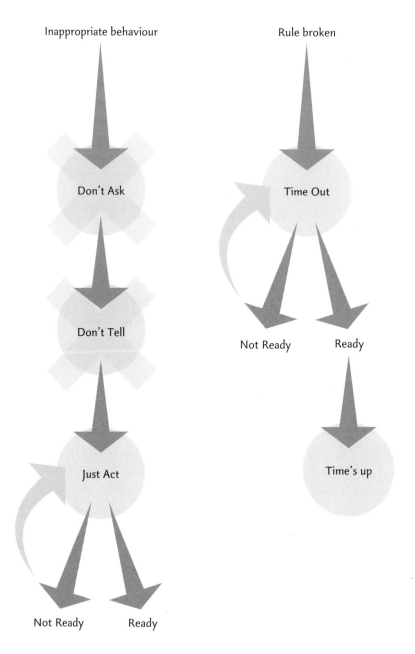

Inappropriate behaviour

Don't Ask

Don't Tell

Just Act

Not Ready   Ready

Rule broken

Time Out

Not Ready   Ready

Time's up

If it happens a third time in quick succession, you are being 'had'. Either stand up to show that 'lap time is over' or — if you think it is now a deliberate assault — use a cot or some other form of brief and inescapable Time Out.

Toddler and child Time Out

Let's start with . . . our child hits another child — unprovoked. Rule broken — Time Out.

The most powerful way we can do that is silently. Move your child to Time Out without a word and walk away. You can be confident that she doesn't imagine that you have done that because she was being such an angel. I have done this and I know how well it works, but I usually feel obliged to say something.

The second most powerful way, to convince your child that you will not tolerate a particular household rule being broken, is to move your child to Time Out without a word. At the door, you affirm one simple point: 'You know you are not allowed to [whatever it is she is not allowed to do]. I'll be back to see if you are ready to behave.' And walk away.

Avoiding pitfalls

Should you get down to their level? No. You need your full height to show how strongly you mean what you say.

Should you explain why they are going to Time Out? No. We have already done a (theoretical) interview and your child knows that this is unacceptable behaviour. Also, you have no doubt explained many, many times and you still have the behaviour.

Should you re-explain when you release them from Time Out? No. It invites them to go, 'Yeah, yeah, yeah. I know that', and then you have to deal with cheekiness. They know why they are there. You know why they are there. There is nothing else to be said.

Should you ask them if they know why they are there before you allow them to rejoin the family? In terms of children learning the rules of the household, I can see no merit in demanding repetition before release. It just invites the sing-song voice and the side-to-side head motion while they parrot in a bored voice, 'I'm in Time Out because I . . .' We are left trying to pretend we haven't noticed that our child is being out-and-out rude because we cannot bear another performance while we insist on an appropriate tone of voice.

I could be persuaded that when they have enough control of their voice to be able to say why they were in Time Out in a polite, respectful and regretful tone that they have achieved the aim of Time Out, which is an opportunity for them to gain control of their behaviour. However, it does contradict the power of a crisp and no-nonsense Rule broken — Time Out — Ready to behave — Time's up.

On balance, I would far rather we opened the door, said 'Time's up' and walked away.

Liberate the object

Sometimes it is more efficient to liberate the object rather than 'incarcerate' the child.

When your child persists in kicking a ball inside the house, when she is running with scissors, when she is tormenting the cat, when she is holding the remote above her brother's head, it is much easier to 'liberate the object' rather than try to move the child.

Acting in silence is extremely powerful. If you must say something, here are some suggestions:

- *I'll just take that ball out of harm's way.*
- *It's dangerous to run with scissors.*
- *The cat will be so much happier outside.*
- *I'll just pop that remote on the fridge so it isn't annoying anyone.*

If you have confiscated a toy that was being used inappropriately, usually 'out of sight is out of mind', but if you want to take a timed approach, set the timer for ten minutes. When it beeps, announce 'Time's up', and return the toy to its original place. It is most likely that your children have moved on and you are saying 'Time's up' to yourself.

How long till they're ready?

We are teaching our children that, when they behave within the rules of the family, they are welcome to all the freedom, goods and services that come with being a family member.

When they break the family rules, they are excluded until they have changed their minds and are ready to behave according to the rules of the family.

Some children can call out or come out when they are ready to behave. Others need you to invite them out. The question of 'How long?' is based on when you experience their change of heart. This may involve remorse. It may involve a perceptible change of attitude. It may involve a willingness to take responsibility for their actions. It may involve a readiness to apologise with sincerity.

A story from home

At the moment of writing this book, my grandchildren are respectively three and a half (Zack) and two and a half (Dani). Zack is more often than not a kind brother and plays nicely with his sister. Occasionally, he has the urge to shoulder her to the ground. He doesn't actively walk up and push her. He 'happens' to run past and connect shoulder to shoulder so that Dani is lying on the ground crying.

A few weeks ago, they were playing in the garden at our place — mostly very nicely, but occasionally with shouldering. Grandma had had enough. The next time Dani was lying on the ground crying, I moved Zack to the edge of the garden. Holding him with a hand on each shoulder, I said, 'Zack. You know you are not allowed to hurt Dani. We are going to stay here till you are ready to be kind to Dani.' We stayed there for what seemed like an eternity but probably was about forty-five seconds. 'I am ready,' said Zack and, unasked, went over to Dani, said 'Sorry' and hugged her.

For about ten minutes, all went well. They played nicely. Zack managed to run past Dani several times. Then again, Zack shouldered Dani to the ground.

Success or failure?

The first question to ask is 'Was this a success or a failure?'

Was it a failure because Zack repeated the undesirable behaviour? I don't think that is fair. If we imagine that one episode of Time Out can fix anything permanently, we are pitching our expectations too high.

For ten minutes, Zack managed to restrain himself, play nicely with his sister and pass her, leaving a safe distance between them. I call that a success — but a success that required repetition.

So, for a second time, I moved Zack to the edge of the garden. Holding him with a hand on each shoulder, I said, 'Zack. You know you are not allowed to hurt Dani. We are going to stay here till you are ready to be kind to Dani.' Again, after a while Zack said, 'I am ready', and was released back to play.

Who's ready?

This time Zack's self-restraint lasted for a longer time but eventually he found it irresistible to skittle Dani for a third time. I removed him from the scene and repeated the same phrases. No sooner had I got to the word 'ready' than Zack declared, 'I'm ready.' My response? 'Well, I'm not and we are going to wait here till I am ready to have you back playing with Dani.'

Being Ready is a two-way street. Sometimes Ready means our child is ready to return to the family and behave according to the rules of the family. Sometimes Ready means the parent is ready to allow the child to return to all the privileges and benefits of the family.

YOU BE THE TIME OUT

Let's look at an older-child example. When our child is too old, too tall, or too physical for us to say 'Go to your room', Time Out is just as useful a response, but *we* need to be the Time Out.

Let's imagine that your child is annoyed with you over something and speaks very rudely to you. Front up, stand your full height, look her in the eye and say very strongly, 'You know you shouldn't speak to me like that. Let me know when you are ready to speak civilly', move away and do whatever it is you need to do. (I have avoided saying 'Let me know when you are ready to apologise', because of the ranges of responses to a request to apologise. More about this later.)

How can we 'be Time Out' as long as is necessary? Just by going about our own work, attending to what needs to be done and not connecting with our child on any emotional level. If mealtimes arrive, we should still invite/allow them to join the family at the table — or send a plate to them if we are feeling particularly aggrieved — but continue to avoid most interactions with them until they have returned to being polite and helpful.

Assuming that our child has been horrible to another family member or a pet, stand close and tall and tell your child to 'Go away until you are ready to behave kindly'. If we are confident and quietly ferocious, it is highly likely that our child will take herself off, probably muttering all the way.

What if we get an out-and-out refusal to budge? Don't start a battle that you may lose. Go away, regroup your feelings and stay distant until your child shows a definite change of attitude. Sometimes it may take a night's sleep, and often by the morning you will be back to a civilised relationship.

But isn't this sulking?

This is a question that has worried me because I find sulking a horrible behaviour to be around — even when it is me doing the sulking!

This is how I see the difference between a Time Out that involves quietly going about my own business with minimal contact, conversation or service and out-and-out sulking.

When we sulk, we usually make sure that the person who is the object of our rage or upset knows that we are hurt and furious — and so does everyone else around. We generally create an air of hostility and respond to overtures with negativity and resentment. There's lots of emotion in the air so it could scarcely be called emotional distance.

When we are being the Time Out that keeps the problem with the child, where we remain unemotional with quiet dignity, we create a space for our child to reflect on what is going on and eventually to take responsibility for both their actions and our relationship.

What about truly awful behaviour?

On the list of awful and totally unacceptable behaviours that our older child is capable of delivering, I would put such things as swearing at, shoving or striking a parent. These behaviours are way over any limit of any acceptable behaviour and require a strong and dignified response.

Let's start with any child over five who strikes out at you. You are entitled to be shocked and you are entitled to be outraged. It is shocking and outrageous behaviour.

Say very strongly something along the lines of 'I can't believe that you would do such a dreadful thing to a parent' and get away to regroup your emotions. Decide that you are going to have nothing to do with your child (except the basics every child is entitled to — a bed to sleep in, food at regular intervals and access to education) until . . . ? Until you are ready to have her around.

One of the big problems with punishing and grounding is often that we are ready to restore things to normal but we have issued an edict that we are now obliged to carry through. Far better to forget about imposed consequence and punishment and simply stay out of your child's way until you are ready to have them back in your orbit.

If this is a one-off episode that happened out of temper or exhaustion, the odds are high that your child will be back to apologise, sincerely and remorsefully, fairly soon and you are likely to be able to accept the apology.

If this was just the last straw in a string of ghastly behaviour, your child may be ready to apologise way before you are ready to accept it. If this happens, you need to respect her apology and respect your feelings — something along the lines of, 'Thank you for your apology. I am still feeling very hurt and angry, so how about you give me more space?'

What about swearing at a parent?

There is a line between swearing around a parent and directly and offensively swearing at a parent. When a child swears around you, by all means express your annoyance and/or use Time Out to show your disapproval and how unacceptable that sort of language is for you. ('Just go away till you can used civilised language around me.')

Swearing at a parent is another matter altogether. I suggest shock treatment to show your child that you are never going to deliver any goods or services to a child who swears at you.

The strategy I am about to suggest is not acceptable to all parents. If you are prepared to do it, you will be amazed at how effective it can be. If it is not something you could or should bring yourself to do, outrage and distance will work, too.

Brace yourself. I am about to suggest that whatever dreadful language your older child or teen has used on you, you use back. (Because we are in print and because this book will be found in family homes, we will use the term 'stupid cow', which is quite bad enough for a child to use on a parent. More often than not, however, the parents who have approached me for help on this matter are being called a 'f****** b****'.)

Picture the scene. Your child has been getting increasingly rude and offensive. As she turns to flounce out of the room she rounds on you and says, 'You are a stupid cow.' Initially, it takes your breath away. What is a parent to do?

Go away and get quietly busy. Sooner or later your child is bound to come with some small service she needs from you. Reply, quietly and evenly, using the same language she has used on you.

- *'Mum! Do you know where my socks are?' Reply: 'I'm sorry. Stupid cows don't do laundry.'*

- *'Dad! I need a lift to soccer.' Reply: 'I'm sorry. Stupid idiots don't do transport.'*
- *'Mum! My cellphone's run out.' Reply: 'I'm sorry. Stupid cows don't do top-ups.'*

Expect her to wander off shocked and in a daze. That was the last thing she expected to hear coming out of your mouth but she has no one to blame but herself. Leave the problem with her. Sooner or later, she will work out what to do.

It may take several hours or even a day or two (depending on our child's age), but this shock tactic usually works to help our children stay responsible for what comes out of their mouths.

RULE BROKEN — TIME OUT SUMMARY

Whatever the age of our children, they need us to be very clear that some behaviours will not be tolerated in our household. Provided that we are clear and promise ourselves that we will respond swiftly and surely — Rule broken — Time Out — *every* time we get this behaviour, we can be confident that our children will give up these unacceptable behaviours.

The hard part is for us to make up our minds that we will be consistent.

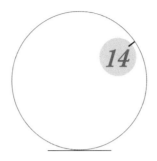

TIME OUT FOR
SIBLING SCRAPS

Before we can sort out sibling scraps, we need to work out what our attitude will be:

- *Is scrapping an inevitable part of having more than one child?*
- *Should children learn to negotiate their own way out of squabbles?*
- *Does the rough and tumble of siblings' physical scraps help them cope with the rough and tumble of real life?*
- *Should we sit them down and help them develop their*

negotiating skills?

- *Will learning to take a tease serve them well when they have to cope with playground hassles?*
- *Do we dread that split second of silence before the scream of pain?*
- *Is their scrapping driving us crazy?*

There are so many contradicting ideas and opinions that it is hard to give you clarity. The best I can do is to offer you one idea that may help you respond in a sure and consistent way. Provided that we can be consistent in our approach, our children will generally accept it as fair.

In Judaism, there is a concept Shalom Bayit — 'The peace of the household'. The implication is that it is good to dwell in a peaceful household and that it is incumbent upon all household members to maintain the peace of the household.

How do we achieve that elusive peaceful household?

THREE STRATEGIES

There are generally three sorts of situation we find ourselves in with respect to the interaction of the siblings in our household:

1   Someone (or several 'someones') runs to you upset.

2   You see physical or verbal unkindness.

3   You can hear that the temperature is rising.

If we are to keep our household peaceful, we need to support ruffled feelings, stop inappropriate behaviour and try to become proactive rather than reactive.

Someone runs to you upset or angry

If there is no blood or teeth marks, you don't need to worry about anyone other than the child in front of you — and that child has just done a very sensible thing. He has got out of a dangerous situation. This is just the sort of decision you hope your teen will make!

Ask what happened and let him tell you his tale of woe. Remember your purpose is to help him settle his feelings so that he can make a wise decision. He might decide to return and play; he might decide to find his own amusement. Either way, he has protected himself and got away before damage was done to him or he was provoked into doing damage. No further action needed.

Some children will want you to take over the problem: 'What are you going to do about it, Mum?'

Don't be seduced into problem solving. Mutter vaguely, 'I'll have to think about that very carefully', and be sure not to intervene. The solution has already been found by your child. It is an excellent idea to get away from people who are being unkind or unfair to you.

They both descend upon you

What can we do when two or more upset children descend upon us determined to dob the other in? Often we are overwhelmed with having to make a judgement based on hearing both sides of the story. When we get into that state, we tend to say things like, 'Just go away. I don't want to hear about it.' This tends to leave our children bereft of support.

Bearing in mind that there are two children — or more — needing our support, how can we hear two people out simultaneously? The obvious answer seems to be to plant a child on either side of you and first hear one story, then the other — that way both children's feelings will be settled and you will be able to help them resolve the conflict. It looks good on paper, but I have rarely been able to get it to work effectively.

Very few angry or upset children can tolerate listening quietly and respectfully to 'the other side'. Watching a parent listening respectfully to 'the other side' is usually more frustration than many children can bear.

I have achieved far more success with agreeing that I want to hear what everybody has to say and going to visit each of them in turn in their bedrooms. This gives us a chance to fully listen to each child without the pressure of wondering about or coping with how the other one is doing. Almost always, by the time you have completed two or more separate visitations, the anger and upset in your household has calmed right down.

Telling tales

Isn't all this encouraging our children to tell tales? It seems part of our Kiwi mentality that 'telling tales' is a far greater crime than hurting, teasing or bullying. With this attitude, it makes the child who seeks comfort or support the person in the wrong.

As a parent or teacher on playground duty, I need the information an upset child brings me. Only with this information can I decide whether my help is needed to get a child out of trouble, my authority is needed to get a child into trouble or my support is needed to soothe a child's upset or to repair physical damage.

By encouraging a 'don't tell tales' mentality we risk leaving vulnerable or hurt children unprotected and bullies free to continue their totally unacceptable and potentially dangerous and damaging behaviour.

Do tell tales and let the adult make a wise decision (which may be as simple as 'This child needs a cuddle') about the information.

You see unkind behaviour

Whenever you see unkind behaviour, whether verbal or physical, send the miscreant away — Time Out.

What if we didn't see what happened? It doesn't matter. Firstly let's deal with what we see in front of us. Our child has broken a household rule. Rule broken — Time Out.

What about the child who is smart at setting up a situation and then melting into the background as soon as we come thundering in, so that the other child is the one caught in the middle of retaliation? If that child is smart, we need to be smarter. We need to get very talented at showing up a bit earlier, so that we catch the child who sets things up.

When we hear trouble brewing

The best time to intervene is when our children are just beginning to get agitated. Most of us are busy doing several of the tasks of parenthood when we hear the situation just starting to hot up. We fervently hope that this time, if we stay out of the way and don't let on we are listening, the children will sort it out by themselves and the disagreement will melt away. I would call that 'the triumph of hope over experience'.

Pretty soon, there is a bang, a crash, a scream — and we have a 'situation' that needs major intervention.

Here is a more successful strategy: stay alert and listen to the sound of your children playing together. As soon as you hear it beginning to 'hot up', show up in the room where they are.

Avoid getting caught up into what is going on, who had the piece of equipment first, whose toy it was in the first place. You really don't want to get into listening to each side of the story and deciding who was right and who was wrong.

Instead, I suggest that you make a no-blame statement, such as 'This isn't working', and split them up. 'You go into your room; you go into your room. I'll set the timer.' At the end of ten minutes, call out 'Time's up' and leave it to your children to decide if they want to regroup.

After you have done this a few times, your children will listen out for your footsteps. (You may want to stomp down the hall to give them an even chance.) Either they will learn not to fight, or they will learn to fight very quietly so you don't interrupt.

THE PEACE OF THE HOUSEHOLD

By refusing to let our children scrap, we are holding them responsible for the peace of the household. By supporting their feelings when they are upset, we are giving them a safe haven to sort out what to do next. By stopping any inappropriate behaviour that we see happening in front of us, we are holding our children responsible for their individual actions, regardless of 'who started it'.

In all of these situations we are keeping out of a vicious cycle and keeping the responsibility for problem solving with each child.

TAKING TURNS

One of the skills of social play that some children do naturally and some children need to be taught is the art of deciding who is going first, the art of taking turns, and a system for timing how long a turn will be.

When our children know how to set up systems for all of these, they will develop rules of play that will stand them in good stead in social situations at home, at other people's places or at school. Teach them how to toss a coin or to draw straws to decide who starts and who goes next. Arrange for them to use some sort of timer (from egg timers for little ones to stove timers for bigger ones or cellphones for teens) to self-regulate how long turns will be.

Play board games and card games with them and model the art of being a gracious winner and a cheerful loser.

WHAT ABOUT OTHER PEOPLE'S CHILDREN?

What are we entitled to and responsible for doing when it is other people's children causing a disturbance in our household? Much the same rules apply: comfort a distressed child, 'exile' a badly behaved child, get in fast and separate them if it is 'hotting up' and make sure the systems are transparent and fair.

What about out-and-out inappropriate behaviour — hitting, biting, snatching and general unkindness? If it is our child, we can unhesitatingly use Time Out. We are often not entitled to remove another child but, having removed our child, we can turn our attention to the child who is not ours and say, with a suitable tinge of unfriendliness, 'I suggest you sit over here and draw quietly with these pens.' While it may not look like Time Out, I am sure the child will be delighted to stay out of your way for a while.

By far the most effective way of dealing with scraps that involve our and others' children is to get in fast at the earliest opportunity and change the activity — possibly to one in a spot where you can keep a closer eye on them.

HIGHLY COMPETITIVE CHILDREN

Many parents find it very distressing to be part of a household of competitive children where everything gets turned into a battle for supremacy. Who gets first to the best chair, the best spot in front of the TV, the favoured seat in the car, the control of the remote, the first into the house . . . almost anything can be turned into a vicious struggle to be first.

Sometimes we are guilty of starting it as an easy way of gaining compliance. 'Let's see who can be dressed first.' 'Who can get into the bath first?' 'Who can finish their breakfast first?' Sometimes our children just seem to be born that way.

When we have highly competitive children, it is really important that we have transparent systems that everyone can see are fair and where everybody knows their turn will come. I recommend sticking up one child's name on the fridge. For that day or that week — whatever works for you — that child is allowed to choose (within the bounds of ordinary household rules and safety) which chair, which car-seat, which TV programme, who goes in the door first . . . whatever decisions are appropriate for a child that age to make. The next day — or week — put up another name on the fridge and that child has 'first choice'.

All you have to do is remember whose 'day' it is. This teaches children to tolerate the frustrations of not always being first, to wait for their turn and to know that their household operates with fair systems and not 'survival of the fittest, the strongest, the noisiest or the most easily upset.'

SIBLING SCRAPS — SUMMARY

When we use a combination of support, boundaries and transparent systems, we can lessen tensions, teach our children good social skills and begin to enjoy the pleasure of children who are nice to be around.

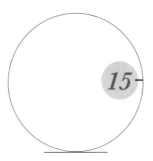

TIME OUT OR EMOTIONAL SUPPORT?

Earlier we looked at using both Emotional Support and Emotional Distance — Boring Cuddles and Time Out — to help us and our children to be part of a peaceful household.

Mostly it is very clear whether we should be going towards support (closeness) or distance. Sometimes it is really hard to tell which way to jump.

When we experience a certain piece of child or adolescent behaviour, it is a good idea to pause momentarily and check how we are feeling about that behaviour. If our response is 'Poor little thing', the odds are high that we are dealing with a child who needs our Emotional Support. If our response is 'You little . . . (let's say) toad', the odds are high that our child is going to need some Emotional Distance to be able to calm her own feelings and be ready to make an appropriately wise decision.

Our child is upset, annoyed, non-compliant, breaking household rules

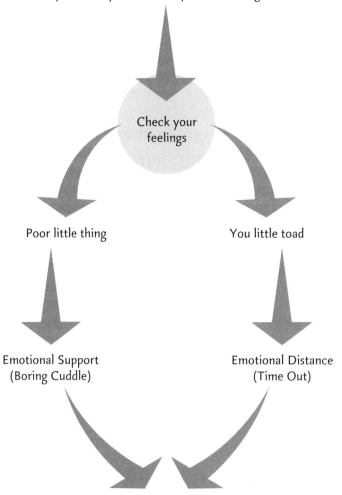

Check your feelings

Poor little thing

You little toad

Emotional Support
(Boring Cuddle)

Emotional Distance
(Time Out)

Our child is able to settle his/her feelings, think through a
wise decision and act appropriately

Sometimes it is hard to read a tired, exasperated, grumpy child. I favour asking the child. For a younger child: 'Do you need a cuddle or do you need a bit of time alone?' For an older child: 'Do you need a hug, do you want to talk about it or would you rather go and have some space?'

Assuming that they stalk off for some time on their own, we need to remember to be the grown-up. Instead of calling, 'Fine, then. Be like that', it would be a more mature response to call to their retreating back, 'If you need that hug or want to talk about it later, feel free to come back.'

Whichever way we decide to go, support or distance, we have the same aim in mind. We are trying to stay out of a vicious cycle of arguing, cajoling, explaining, distracting, threatening and punishing. Instead we are supporting our children's feelings or refusing to accept inappropriate behaviour in such a way that our children have no option other than to settle their feelings (whether by cuddle or Time Out) so that they can get into thinking mode about what would be an appropriate action.

WARM SPACE

Usually, we tend to think of Time Out as a 'cold' space, with the absence of parental support. However, there are often times when a bit of space to get away from the pressure, calm their feelings and order their thoughts is just what our child may need.

After kindergarten, school, work or a hectic party, our children may need time to themselves. Some children can just take the sort of space that they need, others seem to have to get bad-tempered or non-compliant first before we or they recognise their need for some down-time. Hence the idea of asking them 'Do you want to talk about it or do you need space?' is both respectful and smart parenting.

Warm space for older children

Often Vernon and I were a temporary haven for disgruntled friends of our teen children. Any of our children's friends were welcome in our house and I would hear our children saying, 'You can stay here as long as you like. The rule is that you have to let your parents know that you are safe. Are you going to ring them or do you want my mum to?' It seemed the perfect compromise for the child who needed to get away and the parent who had concerns for their child's safety and wellbeing.

When our older daughter, Tanya, reached her mid-teens, she would occasionally find us impossible to live with. She would stalk out of the house in the morning saying, 'I can't live here any more', but would always add, 'I'll ring you to let you know where I am.'

In the afternoon we would get a call from her — at a friend's house, ostensibly to 'work on a project' — and the conversation would usually go along the lines of, 'You know I can't bear to live with you all. I'm staying here.' I would have to work hard on myself to be very controlled and say, calmly and warmly, 'You take all the time you need and when you are ready, we'll be pleased to have you home.' She would usually say, rather grimly, 'It can't be tomorrow.'

During the day, I would speak to the mother of the house who was always a little surprised that neither child had let on the real reason why Tanya was there. She would undertake to look after Tanya and I would undertake to reciprocate if ever there was a need.

It usually took three school days and two nights away and Tanya would show up and we would be pleased to have her back. Episode over till the next time!

GETTING IT WRONG

It is inevitable that, at times, we will make a wrong call. We will offer support to a child who needs space, or insist on Time Out for a child who needs support. No worries. Retreating to the other side is relatively easy.

Your child seems upset and angry. You approach your (younger) child with, 'Are you a big girl who needs a cuddle?' only to be met with 'Go away. You're a poo-bum!'

It is not very hard to move from Emotional Support to Emotional Distance. Leave her alone until she is ready to ask for a cuddle or ready to just get on with life.

You approach your (older) child with, 'You seem very angry and upset. Would you like to talk about it?' The startling response is a snarled 'Go away. Why do you always have to stick your nose in?' Beat a hasty retreat. Let your child have as much space as she needs. Hopefully, she will return to apologise for snapping at you and, if you are extra lucky, she will seek your advice about whatever was bothering her in the first place.

If she doesn't wish to discuss something, respect that. If you have to intervene, own your need. 'I know you don't want to discuss this, but I am worried that . . . I'd like to tell you my concerns. Can you handle that?' If the answer is still 'No', she wouldn't hear what you have to say anyway. Save your breath.

The other way we can head off in the wrong direction is when we have made a request and our child has declined and gone to Time Out. After a while we hear the sound of a child dreadfully upset. Time to offer Emotional Support. Go in and, if it is not dangerous, rub her back or offer a cuddle. Soothe her feelings and pretty soon she will share with you what is bothering her. Once that is done, she will most likely be ready to comply with the original request.

SHY CHILDREN

It is often hard to know how we should respond when our child is exhibiting the sort of behaviour that comes under the general heading of 'shy'. The sorts of behaviour that tend to lead us to use this word range from a rather charming natural reserve to a refusal to meet, greet, thank and farewell. Should we regard these behaviours as part of our child's personality, therefore something we cannot do anything about, behaviour that requires our support or behaviour that requires us to take a stand? My answer tends to be 'All of the above'.

Since I am of a very outgoing and rather noisy temperament, I find the reserve of the shy person rather refreshing and attractive. Children with natural reserve like to observe and size up a situation rather than throw themselves into it without care or forethought. This is a highly sensible approach and our children who operate this way deserve our support. For some unknown reason, many people find this uncomfortable and put a lot of effort into trying to force unwilling children to join in right from the start. In these situations, it is our job to put an arm around our child and say supportively and encouragingly, 'Jenny is just watching and waiting till she feels comfortable to join in. I'm sure she'll be ready quite soon.'

Meeting, Greeting and Thanking

Meeting, greeting and thanking are social skills that we need to initially model, then encourage and eventually insist upon for all our children, outgoing or reserved. An appropriate rule for most households is that our children meet and greet people on arrival and say goodbye when they depart. At other people's houses, they need to meet and greet and then say 'Thank you for having me' when they depart.

Our outgoing children are capable of these basic good manners from the middle of their third year. Even with our very reserved children, we can insist that they do 'the basics' with people who are familiar to them by the time they are three.

Check your feelings. When you have moved from 'Poor little shy child' to 'Little toad', it is time to take a stand. When familiar family members or good friends come over, expect your child to say 'Hello' to them and not to the carpet. If your child refuses (and don't be sucked into an 'I can't' which actually means 'I won't') she can wait in her room until she is ready.

Similarly, when you go out to a friend's or relative's home or to a familiar kindergarten, your child may need to wait in the car or on the doorstep until she is ready to greet appropriately.

Don't agonise over a refusal to say thank you upon leaving. Pop the child in the car, say a brief and strong, 'I am very cross. You know that you are expected to say "thank you for having me"' and drive home in thunderous silence (otherwise known as Time Out). If you live less than ten minutes away, you might get home still so cross that your child needs to wait in her room while you unpack the car v-e-r-y s-l-o-w-l-y.

GRIZZLING, WHINING AND WHINGING

One of the sounds that can turn an otherwise loving parent into a dangerous, snapping monster is the ongoing grating sound of their child grizzling, whining, whinging or all three simultaneously with no apparent reason or solution. We can use this model of 'Which way to jump?' to bring an end to what feels like perpetual grizzling.

Our first thought should be 'Can I offer support to a miserable child?' Put your arms out, saying, 'You look really, really, unhappy. Would a cuddle help?' Sit down and pretend to yourself that you are there all day and you have nothing else that you would rather do. Stay still and stay as present as you can. Once the grizzling has subsided you may be able to invite your child to join you in whatever work you are doing. (If you are working at the sink, a high-chair or a kitchen ladder is great to keep your child near you but safe.)

If the grizzling starts up again, offer another cuddle and give it wholeheartedly. If the grizzling is about a child feeling off-colour or generally miserable, long and very Boring Cuddles are often the answer. But it does have limits.

Sometimes the whining seems to be about nothing at all and your feelings are changing from 'Poor little thing' to 'If this goes on for twenty seconds more, I think I will . . .' If you are starting to think vengeful or dangerous thoughts with regard to your beloved child, the odds are very high that you should be moving from Emotional Support to Emotional Distance.

Go close to your child and give one warning, 'You need to stop that noise — right now.' If the noise doesn't stop, scoop your child off to her room and say very firmly, 'When you have stopped making that noise, you are welcome to join me in what I am doing.'

BEING A 'GOOD SPORT'

One of the most important skills we can make sure our children have is the ability to be both a gracious winner and a gracious loser. For some children, we don't have to make any effort. Their innate social skills, their eagerness to be part of a group, their willingness to play games for the sheer delight of being with their friends, means that the give-and-take of playing games comes easily to them.

Others find the tension of losing or not being good at particular games almost unbearable. If they cannot hit the ball, if they cannot run the fastest, if their counter goes down the snake, their world comes to a crashing halt. They may refuse to take part, they may need to run off, they may throw the board in the air and if we try to block them from doing so, they may become aggressive.

What is a parent to do? My first recommendation would be to err on the side of empathy and warm space. Put an arm around her and say something that shows her you really understand how dreadful she feels. 'It's really hard when you can't make the ball go where you want it to.' 'You find it awfully hard when you are not the fastest runner.' 'You find it really hard to lose, don't you?' 'You get really upset when the game is not going your way.'

Depending on how that goes — and how much you are needed to keep the game going with the other players — you may wish to say, 'Now let's just sit over here together till you are ready to join in.'

If you are unable to stay with her, you might say, warmly, 'Now! I need to get back to helping the others. Would you like to have a bit of a breather and come back to the game when you are ready?'

If Emotional Support or Warm Space is not doing the trick, or if the behaviour is entirely unacceptable (i.e. she hurts another child or destroys a piece of equipment), Time Out may be the best way to go: 'Go and take a five-minute cool-off time. I don't want to see you back until you are ready to behave appropriately.'

HOMEWORK HASSLES

For some of us, the time after school when our child, willingly or with a small amount of reluctance, gets 'stuck into' her homework, can use our support or our advice, completes the work in a reasonable amount of time and gains some satisfaction from a job well done, can be a pleasant and productive part of family time.

For others, homework time can be one of the high-stress points of the day — one that we dread the thought of and cannot wait to be over. What are our options?

Let's talk about what we should try to avoid. Let's try not to get into the vicious cycle of explaining, nagging, cajoling, threatening, yelling and punishing. What else is there to do?

My first shot would be to see if there is some way we can support our child through something she clearly finds difficult. Break down her work into a checklist of achievable small tasks that she can complete. Or say to her, 'I know you find some of this homework really hard/tedious/boring but we need to get it done. Which bits would you like me to help you with?'

At the end of a tiring school day, give her some leeway. If she asks you how to spell a word (unless you are in the middle of testing her spelling), just spell it out. I know of no better way to begin a half-hour war than to say to your child, 'Look it up in the dictionary.' If she just wants you to sit near her while she writes a paragraph, if you possibly can, do so.

On the other hand, don't sacrifice reasonable behaviour for the sake of getting the homework done. Just because she finds homework a difficult chore, you shouldn't put up with rudeness or stalling behaviour, and there is no reason why she should be taking out her frustration on you or on any convenient siblings.

If you need to, don't hesitate to say, 'This isn't working. You go off to your room and come back when you feel ready to do your homework.' You will be amazed how ten minutes alone in a boring spot will make homework look like a far more attractive option.

If you have had a couple of shots at getting through the homework and you feel yourself being strung along with every excuse and delaying tactic under the sun, remember that you have limits on your time: 'I only have another quarter of an hour when I am available to help with homework. Are you going to use my help wisely or are you spending part of the time in your room?'

Remember that you should exercise your magic power of 'to sign or not to sign' the homework notebook. If you are being strung along, don't hesitate to write, 'Georgia was unable to complete her homework.' There may even come a time when you write, 'Georgia refused to complete her homework.' Don't threaten. Just do it. Your child will be stunned.

Bear in mind that there will be some days — hopefully rarely — where your child will simply be too exhausted to complete her homework. Don't hesitate to support her with a note that reads, 'Georgia was too tired to complete her homework tonight. She has undertaken to complete it tomorrow.'

With a matter-of-fact attitude that homework is part of a regular after-school routine and a flexible combination of Emotional Support and Time Out, it should be possible to develop good homework habits in our children.

TO SUMMARISE

Time Out can only be effective in a climate of Emotional Support. By being prepared to make your best guess, based on your feelings towards your child at any given moment — and provided that you haven't got other major annoyances or worries that are clouding your judgement — deciding whether to support or distance gives you the flexibility to put your children in a position where *they* can make an appropriate decision.

And if you wish to change your mind, the odds are that the situation has changed and requires your flexibility to move to another position.

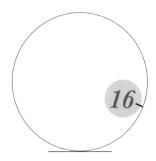

FREQUENTLY ASKED QUESTIONS ABOUT TIME OUT

Whenever I give a parenting seminar there are questions that almost always pop up. When they happen during a seminar, it is easy to sidetrack and address them on the spot. While writing this book, some sidetracks haven't fitted in easily, so I have collected some of the most frequently asked questions here.

I have also collected some of the questions that people often ask at the end of a seminar on child behaviour about eating, sleeping or toilet-training hassles.

WHERE DO I START?

Parents often ask me how they should go about implementing changes in their households:

- *Should they warn their children that there will be changes?*
- *Should they start by holding a family meeting?*
- *Should they start by sitting all the children down and explaining the rules?*
- *Should they post the rules on the fridge or the notice-board?*

I am not in favour of any of these approaches. Emotional Support, compliance with household rules and compliance with simple requests are not things that we need to discuss with our children. These are parenting decisions, made by parents for the wellbeing of their children. We don't need to obtain their agreement — it is going to happen anyway.

By telling them what we are planning, we may inadvertently invite discussion and pretty soon we may find ourselves defending, persuading, cajoling and, ultimately, arguing and shouting. Support and compliance are not up for discussion. Why would we want to give away our game plan?

However, don't suddenly implement all the changes late in the afternoon when everybody is tired and on a short fuse. Instead, I recommend starting at the beginning of the day as you intend to proceed. Insist on compliance, act swiftly when household rules are broken and give emotional support where necessary.

When they come home from kindergarten or school that day, make sure that they return to the same household that they left in the morning — a household that puts limits on inappropriate behaviour, believes in compliance with household rules and provides support for tired or upset children.

You are on your way.

BUT IF I RESPOND TO EVERY NON-COMPLIANCE, WON'T HE SPEND ALL DAY IN TIME OUT?

If we think in terms of taking care of each behaviour one at a time, it is no wonder we fear that our non-compliant child will be in Time Out all day. A better way of thinking about it is to think of ourselves setting boundaries around inappropriate behaviour (including non-compliance and the breaking of household rules). That way, our children understand that the rules that they already know exist, plus the expectation that they will do as their parent asks them to, apply all the time.

If you start the day as the boss and insist that your first three requests are complied with, or deal promptly and firmly with the first three times your child breaks a household rule is dealt with promptly and firmly, you will be amazed at how smoothly the next few hours go. Similarly, when your child comes home from preschool or school, be sure your first three requests are met.

How does this play out in practice?

Request one: Getting dressed

Expect your child to start the day suitably dressed (whether you dress them or whether they dress themselves). Don't let them out of their room until they are dressed. If they start mucking about, just say, 'Let me know when you are dressed/ready to hold still while I dress you and then you are welcome to join the family.' Go about your morning tasks, until he lets you know he is ready.

Rule broken: Your child hits a sibling

Put him straight in his room and tell him you will be back to see if he is ready to behave. Go and do one of your morning tasks. Pop back to see if he is ready to rejoin the family.

Request two: Tell him to go and clean his teeth

You follow up a few minutes later and find him in his room playing with the dog. Remove the dog and tell him he is welcome out when he is ready to brush his teeth.

All this may take longer than usual but, by the time he has experienced his third Time Out for the day, he is under no illusion that you intend him to do as he is told. The rest of the morning is bound to be much smoother.

This answer always leads to the next question:

BUT WHAT IF I AM IN A HURRY?

We all want the magic parenting trick that will work when we are under time pressure. If I knew what it was, I would not only share it — I would market it! Parenting isn't like that. It is a lifelong process of supporting feelings and holding boundaries on the journey of raising our children to become competent, independent young adults.

Children sense when we are in a hurry and when we are vulnerable. I don't think they deliberately set out to make our lives difficult; I think that they thrive on firm guidelines and, when we start to falter, they seem to take over (not very wisely) the management and create trouble.

The best option is to follow the guidelines laid out in Chapter 10 where we keep the problem with our child, and make sure that the child who makes the family run late carries the penalty. Instead of running around frantically trying to make your child hurry up, leave him be and get yourself ready (see pages 100–101).

Of course there will be times when you simply don't have time to see things through. Sometimes you can come back to the issue when you return home later. Sometimes you just have to let it go. Sometimes it is wiser to let things go.

As long as you are insisting on compliance most of the time, you are meeting your childrens' expectation that you, not they, are running the household.

WHAT ABOUT TIME OUT WHEN I AM IN SOMEONE ELSE'S HOME?

There is always a spot you can use. You can take your child to another room and leave him — or, if that isn't appropriate, you can stay there silently with him. You can put him in his car-seat. You can pop him on the back doorstep. If it is winter, hand him a jacket.

Remember it doesn't matter much where. Time Out is our state of mind which shows our child that we are not prepared to let the bad behaviour continue; we are going to take prompt action; we are not going to enter into discussions; we are going to take our child away from all the fun and action — until he is ready to take age-appropriate responsibility and behave appropriately.

WHAT ABOUT TIME OUT AT THE SUPERMARKET?

Abandoning your shopping and going home has great 'shock value'. However, beware that if it doesn't do the trick the first time, it is only likely to become more and more inconvenient for you and less and less effective for your child. I would far prefer that you insist on good behaviour rather than concede and give up on your shopping.

It helps enormously if you can have two adults, so that when your child behaves badly, one of you can take him to the car and wait till he is ready to behave and the other can continue shopping and looking after the other children.

If bad behaviour happens near the end of the shopping trip, finish as best you can. Silently glowering, put your child in his car-seat. Make one statement about how awful it has been and drive home in grouchy silence. Let the simmering silence in the car be your Time Out.

If you are still cross when you get home (remember, 'check your feelings), say, 'That was a hideous supermarket trip. Now get into your room.' Unpack the shopping and put it away rather slowly. Time's up.

SHOULD I DEMAND AN APOLOGY FOR NON-COMPLIANCE?

Most children realise that their behaviour has been inappropriate and will express contrition. Accept graciously: 'Thank you for your apology'. 'Thank you for doing as asked.'

Some children — particularly our strong-willed ones — may come out of Time Out ready to do as they're told but still smouldering with resentment that they have to. 'All right then. I'll do it.' To ask for an apology at this point is courting disaster. Just thank them for the completed task and stay out of their way while they simmer down. Most children understand instinctively that they should be doing as they are asked. That doesn't mean they like it.

Some children will apologise easily and naturally. With others, it is like trying to drag out their teeth. Often our strong-willed children would rather choke than apologise but, if left to their own devices for a while, they will 'behave apologise'. They may open up a conversation, they may offer some help, they may just hang about pleasantly. I think it is wise to graciously accept their willingness to reconnect and save your insistence that they apologise for situations outside home.

WHEN ONE CHILD HAS HURT ANOTHER, SHOULD I MAKE THEM APOLOGISE?

A child who has accidentally hurt another child will apologise spontaneously and immediately. So we can assume, where an apology is not forthcoming, that it was deliberate. Are they sorry when they have hurt someone deliberately? Probably only that they were caught!

I think that we should also consider the child who has been hurt. Having just been pinched by a particular child, they are likely to feel very uneasy — with considerable justification — if that child comes towards them to give them a forced hug.

On the other hand, some people expect an apology as good social form. If that is what we want it is fine to insist, but we need our child to apologise at least with the appearance of sincerity. In that case, we need to let them know that we expect him to come out of cooling down in Time Out only when he is ready to apologise.

Having made our expectations of a decent apology clear, we should not accept a sarcastic 'Well, sor-ry', nor should we accept an eyes-downcast whisper. Send him back to Time Out until he is ready to apologise properly.

SURELY A CHILD NEEDS TO BE ABLE TO TAKE A TEASE?

Absolutely. If our child cannot cope with the odd good-natured jibe or people poking gentle fun at them, they are going to find social relationships rather difficult.

Sensitive children may struggle to cope with the ordinary physical or verbal rough and tumble of childhood. It is our job to support their feelings and empathise that it is sometimes hard when people make remarks that you find hurtful.

On the other hand, there is a line that is crossed when teasing becomes taunting and I think that it is a parent's job to ensure that we do not permit taunting in our household. What is the line between teasing and taunting? Teasing has a certain mutuality about it. Two people have mutually decided that they will exchange teasing comments and they can both tolerate, if not enjoy, the interaction. It becomes taunting when one person cannot handle the comments.

We can start at home by insisting that our children do not taunt one another nor be verbally unkind. When our child comes home from school, unhappy about how his classmates are treating him, we need to listen with empathy. If this isn't powerful enough, we may be able to help our child think up a few smart, good-humoured answers to have in his arsenal and let him rehearse them at home.

If this isn't powerful enough, your child is probably being bullied and that often requires adult intervention.

I'VE BEEN CALMLY PUTTING HIM IN TIME OUT (FOR HITTING) LIKE YOU SAID AND IT STILL ISN'T WORKING

I know that lots of people say we must stay calm. I agree that it is not advisable or useful to become hysterical or angry and scream and shout. That just means we are out of control and our children experience that as having parents who not are in control.

On the other hand, if we are responding calmly to outrageous behaviour like hitting, we are giving our children the message that their behaviour is not of great concern to us. If, every time our child hits out, we calmly put him in Time Out, he may be experiencing it as some sort of game rather than a serious response to unacceptable behaviour.

I think that outrageous behaviour demands an outraged response. By all means use a quiet voice, but let it show your outrage when you say, determinedly, 'You know you are not allowed to hit.'

I HAVE USED TIME OUT FOR HITTING EVERY TIME AND IT STILL ISN'T WORKING

Somewhere 'out there' we have been led to believe that we should focus on one bad behaviour and ignore the rest. It comes under the heading of 'don't sweat the small stuff'. I really disagree with this (see page 71.) Inadvertently, we may be giving the message that it is OK to be non-compliant but it is not OK to hit. If our children do not respect our authority over lots of things, where is our credibility about the one behaviour that we are trying to change?

Instead of solely thinking about hitting, tackle compliance issues. Begin the day as the boss who is in charge of the family, refuse to tolerate non-compliance or the breaking of any household rule and be extra-vigilant about tackling hitting whenever it occurs. You will not only have a much more peaceful household; you will have a child who respects you and is a much happier person.

WHAT CAN I DO ABOUT MY YOUNG CHILD WHO RUNS AWAY?

The first thing to think about is what his general compliance is like. So far, I have never known a child who is compliant at home to suddenly get an urge to run away when we are out. Why would we expect our child to be compliant out, where there is much less control, when we struggle with compliance at home and have a much greater chance of being in control?

So the first thing we can do about running away behaviour is to start as the boss every day and insist on the first three requests being met — and using Time Out with each one until they are.

The second thing to think about is the point of leaving the house. Is it a struggle to get our child into a push-chair or car-seat? This one isn't even a compliance issue. Imagine me interviewing your child and asking him if he is supposed to sit in his push-chair, walk next to his parent, sit in his car-seat or wear his safety-belt? He knows what he is supposed to do. He is just not doing it.

Regard it as Rule broken — Time Out.

- *You go to put him in his push-chair. He mucks about. Time Out till he is ready.*
- *You go to get in the car. He creates difficulty. Time Out till he is ready.*
- *He makes it difficult to get him into his car-seat. Time Out till he is ready.*
- *He refuses to put his seat-belt on. Tell him the car is not moving till it is on. Sit silently till he is ready. (You be the Time Out.)*

The third part is when you get him out of his push-chair or car-seat. Tell him he has one chance to show you that he can walk next to you. The moment he moves away, catch him and contain the behaviour.

With a child under four, I would put him in reins for the rest of that outing. With a child over four, I would take him back to the car and tell him that you will not let him out till he has convinced you that he will stay appropriately next to you.

Provided that you contain his behaviour at all three stages — at home, at the point of leaving home and when you get out of the car — the running away behaviour should stop.

WHAT CAN I DO ABOUT MY TEEN WHO RUNS AWAY?

One of the situations that I find difficult to deal with on the spot often comes at the end of a seminar on child behaviour, when I have a queue of people lined up to ask individual questions, and a parent or parents approach me with an anguished look. Their teen has run away — I am talking the hot-tempered, short-term sort of running away — and the parents are receiving all sorts of conflicting information about how to respond.

Among the advice that is causing them the most anguish are the recommendations 'Tell him that he can come home when he is ready to apologise', 'Let him come home but only if he is willing to sign a contract to obey the ground rules', or the most upsetting and unwise 'Tell him that he comes home now or he can forget about coming home at all'.

My take is a little different. I believe that we owe our children a minimum of a roof over their heads, food to eat (under that roof), a bed to sleep in and access to education. If they choose not to avail themselves of those, we cannot force them, but they are there waiting for them. We don't need to beg them to come home but they do need to know that home is always there for them.

While they are away and/or upon their return, our primary task is to be available for Emotional Support, give advice only if requested (those magic words, 'What do you think I should do, Mum/Dad?') but not to solve their problems. We can hold our boundaries around what we are prepared to do or not do, but our Emotional Support and a safe roof over their heads is the least we can keep available.

Only once our relationship has been re-established can we begin to insist on some contribution to the tasks of running a household. Sometimes when children have stormed away with a hiss and a roar and have then been graciously welcomed back, they may even feel like being helpful.

I AM HAVING TROUBLE WITH MY CHILD'S SLEEPING/EATING/TOILET TRAINING

At the end of a seminar about 'getting our children to behave better', there is always a line-up of people asking for specific information about eating, sleeping and/or toilet-training hassles. There are complete chapters on these topics in my book *Of course I love you . . . Now go to your room!*, so I am going to confine myself to the intersection of eating, sleeping and/or toilet-training hassles and non-compliance and when, if ever, it is suitable to use any form of Time Out.

If you have tried all the usual strategies and you are still struggling, the first question to ask yourself is, 'What is my child's general compliance like?' If you are using most of the generally advised strategies, if you are supporting your child to learn what for some children is a challenging skill and your child is co-operative and competent for a few days and then somehow 'forgets', the odds are that it is a compliance issue.

Let me put it another way. If I ask, 'What is your child's general compliance like?', I frequently get the answer, 'Oh! Fine! He's a good little boy.' If I then start asking about specifics . . .

'What's it like getting him dressed in the morning?'

'How easy is it to get him to clean his teeth?'

'How about putting on his shoes and socks?'

. . . a different picture starts to emerge. According to the child's response, we start to understand if his way of saying 'No' is Sad, Mad or Distancing.

The next question to ask ourselves is, 'If our child is giving us grief over ordinary compliance, why would we expect him to suddenly get co-operative over eating/sleeping/toilet training?' The miracle is that there are many non-compliant children who do perfectly well with eating/sleeping/toilet training and there are very few children who give us grief with all three.

So my first recommendation is to take care of any compliance issues.

The second part of your action needs to be specific to the particular 'body hassle' we are struggling with.

Is there a place for Time Out with sleep issues?

Mostly, with sleep issues, I favour strategies that support our children to feel safe, secure and part of the family while they go off to sleep. Popping in at increasing intervals (a strategy described fully in *Of course I love you . . . Now go to your room!*) provides them with support and connection.

However, there comes a point in your evening where you just don't fancy having a little pyjama-clad figure showing up in your living room, nor do you fancy your first moments of down-time peace shattered by the sounds of wailing, cackling or thumping on walls.

The version of Time Out that is appropriate and gives your child the option of being ready to conform to the rules of the household is to warn, once only per evening, 'If you come out (or keep being so noisy) your door will be shut for five minutes.' The next time your child steps out of line, shut the door saying, 'I'll be back in five minutes to see if you are ready to stay in bed, be quiet and have the door open.'

Go back five minutes later and ask, from the doorway, 'Are you ready to stay in bed, be quiet and have the door open?' Very few children can resist the opportunity to have an open-door connection with the family — until adolescence, when they opt for the closed door.

If it happens more than three times in an evening, you are being 'had'. Close the door and enjoy your peace.

Is there a place for Time Out for food issues?

If you have read either of my previous books, you will know that I feel very strongly that what a child eats is not a matter for praise or punishment, but should be driven by our children's appetites. You will find ways of handling difficult eaters written up in detail in either *Of course I love you . . . Now go to your room!* or *They look so lovely when they're asleep.*.

My summary of this is, it is our job as a parent to put in front of a child, five times a day, food that our child reasonably likes. It is our child's job to decide what to do with that opportunity (eat or don't eat).

However, it is not our job to put up with bad behaviour at the table, just so that our child will eat. Even with the worst (otherwise healthy) eater, we will not be doing him or us any favours if we let him get away with awful behaviour at the table just so he will eat a couple more spoonfuls.

I don't regard asking to be fed as a compliance issue. At the end of a busy day, I wouldn't hesitate to feed a tired child that requested it. I do regard lolling off the chair, making 'soup' out of all the meal ingredients, tormenting siblings, opening his mouth deliberately to display half-chewed contents and so on, as ways in which our child can destroy any semblance of a happy family meal.

If it is simply that our child has had enough of eating, I would rather take his plate away and invite him to stay as a social (non-eating) part of the family meal. If he is too tired to stay at the family table, I would invite a young child to play nearby.

However, for deliberately broken rules of behaviour at the table, I would unhesitatingly recommend Time Out till he is ready to join us and behave well. I would emphasise the table behaviour rather than the actual eating.

Is there a place for Time Out in toilet-training issues?

There is absolutely *no* place for Time Out while children are becoming aware of when their body needs to wee or poo, mastering the skills of getting to the toilet or potty on time and learning to deal with their clothing when they get there.

However, there does come a point in many parents' lives when they are confident the term 'accident' is a euphemism for 'They know perfectly well that their body needs to go, they know what to do when they get there, they just cannot be bothered stopping what they are doing to get up and go to the toilet in time'. This applies particularly to the child who hangs on and persists in playing on and releasing little bits of wee or poo.

This is a form of non-compliance. Their body needs to go. Their body is sending out warning signals. They are ignoring the signals.

If our child is hopping around doing the 'I'm avoiding the toilet' dance, don't bother getting into a 'Do you need to go to the toilet?' 'No I don't' 'Yes you do' battle. Simply insist your child goes right there and then. 'Your body needs to wee/poo. Let's go to the toilet now and try.' When you get there, park the child on the toilet and count very slowly to twenty. Most children with a full bladder will wee by the time you get to eighteen, tops.

If you discover your child has wet pants, stinky pants (they wee-d a little bit a while ago and it has since dried), skid-mark pants or worse, you need to act powerfully and inconvenience your child sufficiently that, the next time his body sends 'take me to the toilet' signals, he will know that the most efficient use of his time is to go right then.

When you make the wet pants etc discovery, take your child to their room and change them. Then say, 'Now I have a lot of cleaning up to do. You stay here.' Stroll away and do whatever you have to do very, very slowly. When you feel like having them back in your orbit, just open the door and say, 'I've finished.'

IS THERE ANY PLACE FOR GETTING RID OF BAD HABITS THROUGH THE USE OF TIME OUT?

When I refer to 'bad habits', I am referring to all those things our children do as self-soothing activities. These are normal and acceptable in a young child, but are unacceptable in an older child when they have just become unconscious habits that are no longer socially appropriate, such as thumb-sucking, nose-picking and hands down their pants. (Yes, I do know the word 'masturbating' but that seems to me to refer to a deliberate adolescent or adult activity, rather than the more child-user-friendly term 'hands down the pants'!)

These activities are rather harmless, self-soothing and/or exploratory (well, some children do seem to have an entire expedition up their nose!) behaviours that most children do.

However, there does come a point at which they move from socially acceptable to socially unacceptable. The age at which they seem to be socially unacceptable is on the rise, so I am not going to commit myself there. However, if you have come to the end of your tether, if you have tried every positively encouraging and rewarding system you can think of to stop the behaviour, if your child can stop when the reward is great enough, if all you can hear is your voice nagging your child about a particular behaviour, it may be time to take a stand.

It is totally inappropriate for a parent to try to humiliate or embarrass or berate a child for a behaviour that was acceptable when they were little but has now become an ingrained habit.

Avoid the speech about it is their body and they are entitled to do it in private. That is just giving them permission to continue. Instead, tell them that it is time for them to give up that behaviour and that you plan to help them.

Every time you discover them doing this behaviour, they will need to spend five minutes in their room. If they are then confident they can be the boss of their hands, they are welcome out to join the family. Additionally, you may like to put up a star chart that celebrates every time they have managed an hour of being in charge of their hands.

DIANE, IS TIME OUT THE ANSWER FOR EVERYTHING? IS THAT ALL YOU CAN THINK OF?

There are two ways that I would like to reply to this question.

Firstly, Time Out seems to me to be the simplest and most effective way of dealing with behaviours (including breaking household rules and being non-compliant) that our children need to give up. It isn't the only way, but it is efficient and effective and leaves us with lots of time and energy for all the positive, creative, meaningful and playful things I would prefer that we were enjoying with our children.

Secondly, there is a small sector of children for whom Time Out is not the right approach and I am going to address that in the next chapter.

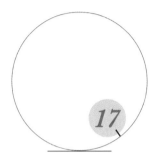

WHEN TIME OUT
MIGHT NOT BE THE
RIGHT APPROACH

This chapter contains a 'health warning': ***Time Out may not be good for your child.***

There is a small cluster of children for whom Time Out (Emotional Distance) from our Emotional Support may be the wrong way to understand and respond to inappropriate or non-compliant behaviour. I would like to tell you the story of how I learned about them.

In the early days of my private practice, I got a call from some foster parents who were caring for a little girl of about three who had just discovered that she had a 'tummy button'. She was tremendously excited about this discovery; the foster parents were mystified at her surprise and joy. They wondered what to make of this and what to do about it.

WHAT COULD IT MEAN?

Initially I was bewildered. Then I started to think about what might lead a child to get as far as three years old and never realise that she had a navel. What other experiences had she never had that most three-year-olds thankfully can take for granted? The little bit I knew about this child's upbringing was that she had a mother who was sometimes able to care for her, sometimes not; occasionally loving, sometimes very angry, often too upset to have the energy to care. Now I know enough to use the term 'intermittently neglected'.

The foster mother and I set up a programme whereby after a bath she would take time with the child to dry and dress her rather as one would a one-year-old. 'Now let's dry your hand, now your little arm, now your elbow and now your tickly armpit' . . . and so on. I also suggested that in the morning when she dressed her, she do it in front of a mirror, so that the child could get a better sense of who she was and what all her body parts were.

As I wondered about what else she may have missed out on, I asked about her knowledge of nursery rhymes, lullabies and other repetitive baby games. She didn't appear to know any of these, so the foster mum spent some time each day doing that. (My reason for choosing this was every culture has nursery rhymes and baby games that not only involve verbal repetition, but often have safe 'frightening' experiences where our child may be upright and then suddenly upside down, or 'peek-a-boo' effects whereby we are there, suddenly we apparently vanish, only to reappear again.)

A few months later, when I was visiting, the little girl did something unacceptable when playing outside and was brought in and put in a corner. After being silent for a short time she began spitting in deliberate anger. The foster dad told me with considerable delight that the child was much improved. Previously, when put in a corner for some misdeed, she had stood there passively, apparently without feelings. Now, when she was put in a corner, she felt both able to and free to show her anger by spitting.

As I continued in private practice, I became aware of a small number of children whom, no matter how carefully the parents followed my suggestions, just didn't seem to comply. The children remained difficult to connect with, reluctant to adhere to the norms of family behaviour, often had great difficulties in relating to their peers, were often quite nasty and their parents never felt that they could quite trust them around younger children or pets.

I LEARNED A NEW CONCEPT

A few years later, I was very fortunate to meet someone who was to become a colleague and ultimately a very good friend. Her name is Judith Morris and through her I have learned most of what I know about the concept of 'attachment'. This is a word used to describe the special capacity to trust that the people responsible for your wellbeing will do their level best to meet your needs. Initially the attachment is to the mother and gradually father, older siblings and extended family. Eventually caregivers and teachers all become people who a child can trust to take care of them, to protect them and to meet their emotional needs.

I began to be aware that many children with whom the Emotional Support/Emotional Distance continuum did not seem to work came from a background of abuse and neglect. This made lots of sense. If they couldn't feel attachment to the people who were supposed to give Emotional Support to them, why on earth would I expect Emotional Distance to work?

Still later, I became aware that there were some children who, from birth, had been part of very loving homes, where they were very well cared for, yet they seemed to show the same lack of response to my suggestions, carefully thought-out, explained and consistently carried through by parents. Now that I know enough to take a more careful history and understand this history in a different way, I notice that there has often been a history of unresolved pain (either emotional or physical — often a combination) in the child's early years.

These days, I explain it to parents in the following way:

The trust cycle

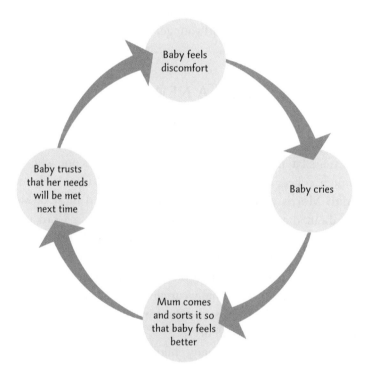

When a little baby begins to feel uncomfortable or frightened, she cries. Mum comes to her right away and does her best to relieve and resolve the upset. She feeds a hungry baby, changes a wet baby, keeps company with a bored or lonely baby, rocks and walks a distressed baby. Pretty soon, the baby feels comforted and trusts that, the next time she is distressed, Mum will show up and sort it out and she will feel better. And so the attachment to Mum, later to be transferred to other trusted people, begins to develop.

Or, to put it in the language that I have been using in this book, the baby learns that when her little emotional tank drains, someone will come and fill it up. Her little tank remains open and available for filling.

When the trust cycle is disrupted

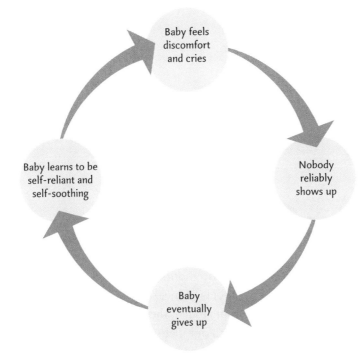

The easiest way to explain the disruption of the trust cycle is to imagine the opposite extreme — the situation when a very young baby is abandoned to a poorly resourced orphanage. (The images I carry in my head are from documentaries about Romanian orphanages under the Ceausescu regime.)

The baby is in a cot and food arrives whenever the timetable says so — provided that there is available food. There may be kindly nurses; there may not. She may be changed when wet or soiled; she may not. There might be a rare time when she is lifted out of her cot and experiences the warmth and support of another person's arms. The baby learns to look after herself as best she can. She rocks repeatedly as the best substitute for comfort that she can manage.

If we think in terms of the baby's emotional tank, the baby gives up on having her tank available for filling, but learns to rely on herself for comfort. She all but seals her emotional tank. She also learns to maximise every opportunity to get whatever she can out of any available adult.

Look ahead to a few years from now when a family comes to adopt this little child and take her home and love her. She will readily accept all the goods or services that come her way, but she may lack the capacity to fully unseal her emotional tank and fully emotionally connect with family members. Since her adoptive parents have opened their hearts and home to her, they may find it very confusing and painful when, even after a number of years of devoted care, their child appears to be manipulative, deliberately hurtful, destructive and after whatever she can get.

Not surprisingly, if the parents use Emotional Distance as Time Out to gain compliance or to stop unacceptable behaviour, they will not get the outcome they expect. At the least, it will not work because the child is expert at and can easily revert to self-soothing or shutting down as a form of self-protection. At the worst, we risk retraumatising our child and they may go off into a 'detached' state of disengagement and dissociation.

No wonder she is not learning anything from it.

If you have adopted a child from a situation of abuse, neglect, trauma or all of these and, after all the love and care you have poured into your child, you still feel as if the child is extra-watchful, extra-manipulative or extra-likely to go off with the nearest stranger who offers them some tiny inducement, I warmly recommend you seek an expert in the field of attachment. They will support you and your child, do one-on-one therapy with your child and give you parenting tips on the best way to handle your child.

This is an extreme example but I use it because it is the easiest way to understand what is going on in our child's head and heart when we have elements of lack of attachment.

MORE LIKELY SCENARIOS

For most of us, our child does not have a background of extreme deprivation and cruelty. Yet some of us may be confused to recognise some of these behaviours:

- *There is a feeling that our child would go off with anyone who gave them 'a better offer'.*
- *Our child has a degree of clinginess that feels extreme.*
- *Our child has an inability to tolerate what seem like ordinary frustrations.*
- *Our child is very superficially engaging or charming — especially to people outside her immediate family.*
- *Our child doesn't seem to 'get' cause and effect.*

- *Our child lacks eye contact with us in the way we would expect.*
- *At times, our child shows an extraordinary lack of compassion.*
- *Our child's cuddles seem to be only on her terms.*
- *Our child's demands for things seems like a 'bottomless pit'.*
- *There are lots of nonsense questions or persistent chattering.*
- *Our child is extremely destructive and uncaring about toys and belongings.*
- *Our child seems to lack impulse control and does things that 'don't make sense'.*
- *Our child lies a lot but does it very badly.*
- *Our child doesn't seem to have developed the sort of conscience you would expect at this age.*
- *They struggle to make friends their own age.*
- *Our child might have uneven learning lags.*
- *Our child likes playing with toys much more suitable for a far younger child.*
- *As the mother, you sometimes find yourself the target of nastiness or dislike, when the father just doesn't experience it that way.*

Before you leap to any conclusions, a lot of these behaviours are commonly found in ordinarily 'naughty' children as well. Also, there are elements of these behaviours in many children who are diagnosed with ADHD, Asperger's and autism.

In order to think about any of these behaviours in relation to our child's ability to form attachments, we need to think about whether there has been anything that might have interrupted the attachment and trust between us and our child.

Have we, as parents, had health or emotional situations that made us less than averagely available to our child?

Has our child had any illness, or have we had any illness, where we have had to be apart from her for any length of time?

Has our child had a lot of chronic pain that we have not been able to relieve? (In New Zealand, many health professionals think of colic and reflux as if they are a normal part of development and that the pain is inconsequential and soon forgotten. The best answer I can give to that is 'Mostly "Yes" but occasionally "No"'.)

Has the child had lots of repetitive, painful medical or related procedures?

Is our child extraordinarily sensitive to noises, smells, or clothing seams or textures or fabrics, how their socks fit, or the texture of their food? Has it been difficult to 'read' what is upsetting them and what to do about it? This has nothing to do with abuse, neglect or abandonment. Their brains just seem to be wired to extra-sensitivity. The problem for them, and for us, is that until we have worked out what is going on, it is difficult to read and believe the cues, so our child may have experienced us as being less than empathetic.

In her first two years has our child had several different caregivers with lots of abrupt changes?

Have we shifted cultures, countries or cities several times? Have some of these been situations where caregivers with a language not understood by our child have taken care of her?

None of these are definitive; many children with abuse, neglect, pain, variable caregiving or any other myriad 'difficult starts' turn out just fine. These are just clues to think about if you have been consistently using Emotional Distance as Time Out and not getting the response you would have predicted.

If you think that there are elements of these in your child's behaviour and background, don't be surprised if Time Out — particularly if you are using it as a punishment — is less than successful. There are, however, some things that we can do that will make life more pleasant between us and our child.

THINK 'BABY EMOTIONAL ATTACHMENT'

One of the loveliest ways to respond to a little baby is to respond to what she is doing or seeking, rather than to lead and teach.

Try this with your child of whatever age. Just be with them and follow the lead of what they want to play or do. Avoid putting in your ideas of how things could be better, higher, smarter or even more fun. Just 'be there' with your child, enjoying the moment of being together.

THINK 'EMOTIONALLY DOWN-AGE'

Particularly after school or kindergarten, or any other time when your child has been away from you and dealing with other caregivers, expect her to be tired and stressed. Come straight home if at all possible and make as few demands as possible (apart from the minimal rules of acceptable behaviour). Be as helpful as you can, e.g. carry your child's bag. Help them take off their shoes and get changed.

Don't be surprised if your child heads for very 'young' toys to play with or makes repetitive sounds or movements. Your child is just finding ways that she knows are soothing for her to get over the stress of a busy day.

Find ways of babying your child in a way that gives you both emotional closeness. Introduce a hand massage or back massage at bedtime, maybe some special songs or lullabies or any other small rituals that are simple, predictable and bring you closer together.

If you have to be away from your child, leave behind a written timetable that shows not only how many sleeps, but also all the meals and all the planned activities — preferably with tick boxes — so that your child can see what will be happening and that you will be coming back.

One of the nicest examples of helping a child to 'hold their parents close to them' while they are away was told to me at a parenting class. (These were parents of a child without any of the challenges that I have been talking about and it is a lovely idea for all parents who need to be away from their children.) The parents had left behind a large hanky. On one corner was a squirt of Dad's aftershave and on the other corner was a dab of Mum's perfume. I am sure that the caregiver refreshed them as necessary.

As with most of our children, expect your child to be difficult to manage upon return and to stick to you like glue.

EMPATHY WHERE POSSIBLE

Wherever it is possible, put into words what your child is feeling, even though it may feel risky or strange to you. Express their annoyance:

- *'Mum and Dad went away and you have been really sad. Were you worried that we weren't coming back?'*
- *'You really find those socks annoying when you can't get the toes just right. Can I help you or do you want another go at it?'*
- *'That smell really upsets you. Let's open some windows.'*
- *'You look like it has been a hard day at school and you want to run around in the playground for a while.'*

If your child needs to be with you, you may even have to notify them when you leave the room. Although this is a pain, it is so much better for your child than sneaking off and hoping that they won't notice or telling them to 'Stay there. I'll only be a moment.' Rather, say, 'I'm just going to the letterbox. [Actually, more likely the toilet!] Do you want to keep playing or do you want to come with me?'

Parents often ask me if this isn't going to make their child even more dependent. Not in my experience. The more you operate at the level of your child's need so that they do not experience unnecessary stress, the sooner they can be assured of your continuous support and manage without your constant support a little more.

Think about the diagram of the partially sealed 'emotional tank'. If we gently keep showing our child we can be trusted to understand her feelings and treat her with gentle and restrained respect, she is gradually going to allow more and more spaces in the seal at the top of her tank.

ROUTINES RULE

Whenever you can have structure and routine, you give your child the security of predictability. Children with attachment issues take a great deal of comfort from knowing how things are going to work and knowing that they are getting it right.

Plans, charts and lists are all things that will make your child's life more predictable.

Recognise that, if you are a parent who values spontaneity and go-with-the-flow, this may be very stressful for your child and is likely to lead to distress and bad behaviour. If you are a 'people person' who craves the fun and company of adults, it may be very hard to drag yourself away — particularly when you can see that there are many other children who can be taken out of routine and become overtired without it leading to a major conflagration.

INCENTIVES WORK

This is a bit rich coming from someone who has just written a book saying 'Give up on praise and punishment'. In my defence, I did say more or less right from the start that my concept of an Effective Time Out was based on Time Out from Emotional Support. To use the 'emotional tank model', this presupposes that your child's emotional tank is open and easy to fill.

Till your child can easily and fully accept all the Emotional Support you have to offer, you are not going to be able to rely on her feeling good inside to be a motivating force. Instead, you will have much more success with 'Grandma's rule'.

Offer the incentive of the chore followed by the reward activity. 'When you are dressed and your bag is packed, then you can go outside and play.' 'First put on your pyjamas and clean your teeth. Then we can have a story.'

Instead of taking compliance for granted and using Time Out for non-compliance as you would with a child whose emotional tank fills easily, you will be helping your child get through her day much more pleasantly for you both if you lead her through her day with a series of tasks and rewards.

CLEAR AND PREDICTABLE CONSEQUENCES

Of course there will be times when your child deliberately does things she knows she is not supposed to do or doesn't do things that she knows she should be doing. You will need to be as calm and dispassionate as you can possibly manage. Respond as if this is 'one of those unfortunate things that happens' rather than getting angry. (You notice that this is the opposite response to a child whose emotional tank is fully open. Then, I have warmly recommended you get outraged and use a strong voice to show your displeasure.)

With a child whose emotional tank is partially sealed, you need to calmly spell out cause and effect without making it personal: 'Because you weren't ready by 8.15, we don't have time to play before school.' 'Because you were destructive with the scissors, you are only going to be able to use them at the kitchen table when I am there.'

TIME OUT CAN BE A CALMING SPACE

Sometimes, if your child is overwrought — particularly if it is as a result of more stimulation or excitement than she can manage — there may be a place for Time Out. This is only a good idea if it calms her rather than annoys her: 'You are so upset and so angry, you need to have a bit of calming-down time.'

CHECK YOUR FEELINGS

Parenting a child with attachment issues is extremely draining and stressful but very rewarding. Also, when we take breaks from our children, they often find it very stressful and we may return to worse behaviour.

Rather than berating yourself for not appearing to manage like other parents seem to, be kind to yourself and lower your expectations. Seek professional help to enable you to understand your child and get through the tough times. Share your concerns and frustrations with reliable friends who will allow you to grizzle.

If you are the parent of a child with attachment issues, you are going to need a lot of Boring Cuddles!

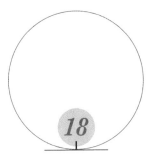

18

A FINAL COMMENT
— EFFECTIVE GROWLING

In Chapter Four I discussed the profound effect Jean Liedloff's book, *The Continuum Concept,* had on my attitude towards raising children, when I first read it seventeen years ago.

What intrigued me the most was that in the entire book there was only one reference to 'growling'. It was rare for a child to do something that annoyed a parent, but when that happened and the parent expressed their annoyance, the child would immediately — and of their own accord — do their best to correct whatever they had done wrong. And that was the end of the matter.

I have often wondered what circumstances I would have to create so that I rarely growled and if I did, it would immediately be effective and my children would not only take responsibility for their actions, but move immediately to correct them.

YEQUANA PARENTING

It seems to me that there are two main factors that create this situation. Firstly, the Yequana babies and infants have their needs for food, sleep, company and exploration met so perfectly that they rarely, if ever, cry and operate very independently from about two years old onwards.

Secondly, the children are totally obedient to parental requests and there is no tension between parent and child. How on earth do they achieve that and is it possible to do that within a Kiwi lifestyle?

SUPPORT THEIR EMOTIONS

To recap the information from Chapter 4, if we behaved like a Yequana Indian, whenever our young child rushed to us upset we would see it as our job to pick them up, cuddle them and do very little else. We would assume that, from the comfort and support of our arms — plus a little walking, back rubbing and muttering of soothing sounds — our child could feel comforted, settle their feelings, reach a point of equilibrium and then wriggle to get down and get on with the next adventure.

When an older child or a teen came to us to tell us about an upset, we could listen carefully to them. We could ask for further information ('And what happened next?') to show our interest and our concern. Further, we could make our empathy clear by small comments like 'How awful for you', 'I'm so sorry to hear that', 'That must have been dreadful for you'.

It is possible that, if we responded to our children with empathy and without criticising or lecturing, they might come to us more often with their problems and would even utter the magic question, 'What do you think I should do?' This would mean that they thought we had something to offer and were seeking the benefit of our experience and wisdom.

It also means that we would understand that some children, after a busy day at school, are simply too tired to talk and prefer to have down-time on their own. We would not only leave them to it, but we would guard their space from their more social and noisy siblings.

TRIBAL EXAMPLE

'That is all very well, Diane,' I can hear you muttering, 'but when do we get to the bit where all a parent has to do is ask and the child rushes to get it right?'

That's the bit I've been struggling with. When a child lives within a tribe, there is a continuous example and expectation of how they are supposed to conduct themselves. If they see children slightly older than themselves consistently behaving in a certain way, they will assume that is what is expected of them and will meet those expectations. How does a single parent or two parents at home manage that?

When a Yequana parent makes a request, it never occurs to the child to do anything other than comply. They have examples all around them of other children doing the same, so compliance seems like normal and expected behaviour. Furthermore, all the adults expect all the children to behave appropriately (and have a common idea of what constitutes appropriate behaviour).

OUR TASK IS TOUGHER

We can do a good approximation of this in our Kiwi homes, but it requires much more effort and determination than that required of a Yequana parent supported by an entire tribe. In other words, initially we are going to work much harder to instil in our children the norms and expectations of behaviour in our 'tiny tribe'.

That's where insisting on certain norms of behaviour, insisting on compliance and the use of Effective Time Out are important.

Once we have asked our child to do something, we need to be clear in our own minds about two things:

> *1* We are not going to weaken our case and lose
>   our dignity by arguing, debating, cajoling,
>   threatening or hurrying them along

> *2* The GST approach: we are not going
>   to provide anything in the way of goods
>   or services until the task is complete.

If we keep our expectation clear that we are not available (not even to encourage — a thinly disguised excuse for nagging!) until the task is done, our children will soon learn that we mean what we say.

SKILLS, COMPANIONSHIP AND FUN

Once we have children who can rely on us for unconditional support when they are upset and rely on us to expect compliance to simple, reasonable requests, we are free to enjoy their company, spend companionable time and work alongside each other.

That way, our children can learn skills from us and with us, they can feel part of a team (or a very small tribe), and they can feel that their contribution is not only expected but also valued.

From my point of view, the reason we are putting so much effort into getting our children to obey ordinary household rules and doing as they are told to reasonable requests is so that they are pleasant to be with. If they are pleasant to be with, we will want to spend more time in their company. There seems to me to be a good case for raising pleasant and responsible children who will be an asset to themselves, to our family, to our community and to our world.

EFFECTIVE GROWLING

None of us likes to be a red-faced, yelling, arguing, screaming parent, nor do we fancy being one who begs, pleads, nags and cajoles our children through the ordinary tasks of childhood and adolescence. It is both undignified and exhausting.

I would love to think that if we are supporting their feelings and firmly and quietly insisting on compliance, on the odd occasion that we growl when behaviour is inappropriate, our children would take full responsibility, 'jump to' and correct whatever they need to.

Nice fantasy or distinct possibility? I believe it is an achievable reality for out tots, teens and everyone in between.